Good
Company

Good Company

THE STORY OF SCOTTISH
& NEWCASTLE

BERRY RITCHIE

Author's Acknowledgements

The author would like to thank the following for their contributions to this book: Peter Balfour, John Dalgety, Henry Fairweather, Sir Alistair Grant, Sir Hew Hamilton-Dalrymple, Dr Jack Harris, Trevor Hemmings, Tim Lewis, Alistair Mowat, Lord Nickson, Michael Pearey, Sir Alick Rankin, Gavin Reed and Brian Stewart. Richard Gibb and Linda Bain were always supportive. Alma Topen of the Scottish Brewing Archive gave generously of her time and expertise. And William Bell deserves special recognition for his energetic and perceptive research.

First Published 1999

© Scottish & Newcastle plc 1999

ISBN

Hardback 0 907383 076

Softback 0 907383 084

Art Director: Hamish MacGibbon

Designer: Robin Farrow

Project Editor: Susannah May

Copy Editing and Index: Conan Nicholas

Published by James & James (Publishers) Ltd

Gordon House Business Centre

6 Lissenden Gardens

London NW5 1LX

SCOTTISH & NEWCASTLE PUBS
AND BREWING TODAY

Photographer: Matthew Weinreb

Front cover: Ale House Interior, by Joseph Parry, 1756–1826
Half-title page: Workers at Newcastle's Haymarket brewery before the Great War.
Frontispiece: Bar 38, Covent Garden, London.

Foreword

Few companies survive for two hundred and fifty years. Even fewer thrive to become market leaders. Scottish & Newcastle is one of these rare organisations. From tenuous beginnings in Edinburgh in 1749, Scottish & Newcastle has grown to be one of Europe's biggest brewing, retailing and leisure groups, with its famous brands sold around the world.

How this has happened is the main theme of this book. Scottish & Newcastle today is the result of the labours of generations of innovative, entrepreneurial and resilient people with the imagination and courage to respond to the vast changes which have occurred in the last two and a half centuries.

It is a very human story, with its full share of dramas. Some of these have been due to personalities. Others have been imposed by external events, some short term, such as crop failures and wars, some permanent, reflecting industrial and social development. This book tells how these pressures inspired the formation of Scottish & Newcastle and shaped its evolution into one of the most successful international corporations in the UK.

Less easy to define is why Scottish & Newcastle has lasted so long and done so well. Anyone reading this history, however, should be left in no doubt that its progress is due to the efforts and talents of the men and women who worked for it in the past and work for it today. This is their story; I thank them for their hard work and congratulate them on their achievement. It is to them that this book is dedicated.

Sir Alistair Grant
Chairman

Tyne Brewhouse, Newcastle.

Contents

Leith harbour, painted by John Thomas Serres.

1

A Potent Fluid

The story of Scottish & Newcastle plc begins in the year of Our Lord 1749 when a 16-year-old youth named William Younger arrived at the port of Leith on the banks of the Firth of Forth, two miles from the centre of Edinburgh, to start work as a brewer.

He came from West Linton, a village twenty miles to the south-west of Scotland's capital, where his father was a farmer who grew barley, brewed his own beer and dealt in wine. There is no record of why he left home. Most likely it was to learn a trade, although maybe young William was getting too big for his boots. But perhaps it was the lure of the big city. The family did not have all its roots in the countryside. William's grandfather had been an Edinburgh lawyer, a Writer to the Signet.

There are few details, either, of William Younger's first job. But what evidence there is suggests that he went to work in Robert Anderson's brewery near St Anthony's Church, Leith.

Anderson was one of the more substantial brewers in Leith, but that did not mean much. Edinburgh was by far the largest city in Scotland, with its population up to around 65,000 thanks to a steady stream of immigrants from the countryside, particularly since Bonnie Prince Charlie's defeat in 1745. But the brewing industry was still small beer, in both senses of the word. Thomas Kirke, an earlier English traveller, wrote of the Scots: 'Their drink is ale, made of beer malt and tunned up in a small vessel, called a cogue. After it has stood a few hours, they drink it out of the cogue, yeast and all; the better sort brew it in large quantities and drink it in wooden queighs, but it is sorry stuff.'

Grizel Sime married William Younger in 1753, soon after he had become an exciseman.

Admittedly, this was outside the larger cities and towns. But it is reckoned that there were fewer than fifty public breweries in the whole of Scotland in 1749. Anderson's average output of 1,500 barrels a year made him one of Leith's bigger producers.

The figure comes from the 'ledgers of brewers liable in payment of the City of Edinburgh's Impost of two Pennies Scots on the pint of ale'. Leith brewers were within the reach of this tax. Nor did they escape the much greater burden of Excise Duties, which had been imposed since the union of England and Scotland in 1707. The arrival of the excisemen following the union had been a great shock to the country's brewers. The VAT men of their day, they proved disconcertingly incorruptible and depressingly energetic, ruthlessly seizing stocks on which duty was unpaid and unscrupulously rewarding informers. Their honesty owed much to enlightened self-interest, as they were paid a percentage of whatever they collected, but that was no consolation to their victims. The only solution was to pay up. Without doubt, it was much more rewarding to be an exciseman than a brewer.

William Younger became an exciseman in 1753, thanks to the patronage of the Honourable Thomas Cochrane, who was a Commissioner of Excise. William's fiancée, Grizel Sime, who lived in West Linton, was a child of the head gardener of a nearby estate belonging to the Earl of Dundonald. Cochrane was the earl's heir and Grizel had been his daughter's playmate when they were both small. His support for the potential son-in-law of his loyal retainer was automatic.

Younger began work for the Excise as second watchman at Leith's recently built glassworks, where he was paid £25 a year to collect the duty

'The De'ils awa' wi' the Exciseman' by Thomas Stothard. Scotland's excisemen were disconcertingly incorruptible and decidedly unpopular among brewers.

on new bottles, a large enough salary for him to marry Grizel. After three years he was promoted to 'Examiner of the County Officers' Excise Books' on £40 a year. A year later and he was an Excise Surveyor of Edinburgh and its precincts, with his pay up to £60 per annum. By 1758, aged 25, he was vigorously confiscating a growing volume of goods of all kinds, from smuggled lace to home-made candles. His main targets were spirits and tea, frequently involving night raids supported by a constable with a warrant, a smith to open locks and a squad of dragoons for protection. Resistance was sometimes fierce and extra troops were brought in from England in 1759 to support the Revenue's officers. But most of the work was less dramatic, involving wearisome searches inspired by information received. William Younger's expenses often included such items as: 'entertainment to two brewers, who we accidentally met at Restalrig, for assisting us in making the seizure (62 lbs of Bohea tea and a cask of brandy) and securing it in the Custom House, being in danger of being retaken.' Less dramatic was the 6s. 6d. he charged for refreshing himself and four subordinates from the exertion of removing two hundredweight of tea from a house in Blackfriars Wynd. All his expenses were scrupulously recorded and witnessed. But they were not an addition to his income. This came from the percentage he was awarded of the money realised on the goods he seized. To begin with these were small; £4 11s. on a cask of brandy, for example. But by the middle 1760s he was receiving commissions as high as £79 on the sale of 6,000 lbs of tobacco, more than his salary for the entire year.

William Younger invested much of his windfall earnings in property. In July 1764, he bought a three-storey house, with garret bedrooms for the servants and a separate coal house, in St Anthony's Place, Leith, which had

William Younger, the founder of what has become Scottish & Newcastle plc. He trained as a brewer before embarking on a lucrative career as an exciseman.

'The Illicit Whisky Still in the Highlands', painted in 1829 by Sir Edwin Landseer, illustrates a typical Highland practice to avoid excise.

A 17th-century brewery, using processes that remained unchanged for 300 years. When Archibald and William II were learning their trade, it was using the same labour-intensive methods.

Archibald Younger, William's eldest son, set up his own brewery at the age of 20 in the grounds of the Abbey of Holyrood House.

been recently built on spec by Robert Anderson. Two years later, Younger purchased a property in the Kirkgate, a few hundred yards away. Next door were 'parts and portions' of a brewery, which he also acquired. In February 1769, he put up 25 per cent of the cost of a piece of waste ground on the north side of Bernard St, close to Leith docks, in partnership with another excise officer, James Brown, a Leith merchant named Alexander Bruce, and an Edinburgh baker called James Craig. The four formed a company to build stables, coach-houses and 'other conveniences' on the land, 'for carrying on the undertaking of stage coaches between Edinburgh and Leith'. Younger also bought an eighth share in a brig named *The William of Leith*, which traded down the east coast to London, and at the end of 1769 he put in the winning bid at the 'publick roup' (bankruptcy auction) of a house at the top of the Broad Wynd, a cul-de-sac running off Shore St, again near the docks.

It was his last investment. Although he was only 37, he was a sick man. In January, he made his will and on 5 May 1770, he died. He left his widow £4,270 Scots, equal to possibly £25,000 sterling today, plus his property and business investments. It was quite an impressive legacy for such a young man. On the other hand, his widow had to support six children, four boys and two girls, of whom the eldest, Archibald, was only 13 and the youngest, William, was just 3.

Grizel Cochrane Younger could not afford to mourn William's death for long. She sold off her late husband's interests in *The William of Leith* and the embryonic stage coach company, and early in 1772 she married Alexander Anderson, another Leith brewer. Archibald became one of his apprentices.

It was a good time to be brewing beer. Plans to build a new town on the open ground to the north of Edinburgh's Old Town had been drawn up in

1752 by Gilbert Elliott, the future Lord Minto. The Nor' Loch had been drained ten years later and the North Bridge had been built across the ravine that was exposed, with a competition to design the First New Town won by another James Craig in 1767. The rectangle bounded by Queen Street Gardens, Princes Street Gardens, Charlotte Square and St Andrew's Square is in essence his layout. By 1770, construction of the infrastructure and housing was well under way. The philosopher David Hume was one of the first to move to the New Town, building himself a house on the corner of St Andrew's Square. Robert Adam and Sir William Chambers, architect of Somerset House in London, designed some of the grandest buildings. The 'second' New Town that followed included the Royal Circus, linked by Great King Street to Drummond Place, and Gillespie Graham's magnificent development of the Earl of Moray's land to the north of Charlotte Square.

Men and materials poured into the city, many of them through Leith. Demand for accommodation, food and beer soared. The Anderson brewery was one of the beneficiaries, as in due course were three of William Younger's sons.

Archibald was the first to set up on his own, leaving home in 1777 at the age of 20, on completion of his apprenticeship, to set up a brewery in the grounds of the Abbey of Holyrood House. Several hundred people lived in the Abbey's precincts, of whom a significant number were involved in the brewing industry because of the availability of abundant supplies of water from wells sunk into the flanks of Carlton Hill. Nine-tenths of Edinburgh's breweries were clustered on the lower ridge of the Canongate for this reason.

Robert Adam, one of the principal architects of Edinburgh's 18th-century New Town.

The Royal Circus, part of Edinburgh's 'second' New Town.

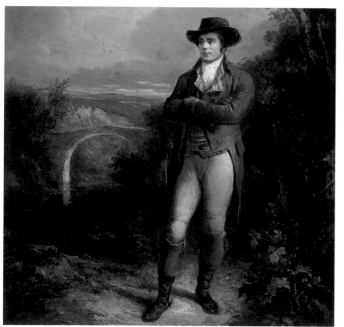

Robert Burns, painted by
Alexander Nasmyth.

Below: John Dowie's tavern in
Liberton's Wynd, reputedly
frequented by Robert Burns.

Facing page: A beer cart in
Grassmarket, Edinburgh, by W.L.
Leitch, c.1984.

One of William II Younger's first
newspaper advertisements.

Archibald Younger soon established a reputation for a quality product. A writer in the *Edinburgh Evening Courant* begged local brewers to produce a better beer than most of the 2*d.* ale on the market. 'Let me exhort my countrymen to brew their ale from the (purest) water, the palest malt and the most fragrant hops, always free from that forced, unnatural strength which the publican finds so advantageous in trade.'

Archibald had the pure water, and he had learned where to buy good barley and hops as an apprentice in Leith, which dominated Scotland's trade with England. Cheap Scottish ale was made from common barley grown in southern Scotland and hardier 'bear' or 'bigg' from the Highlands and the borders. But English barley was acknowledged to be superior to the best that Scotland could produce. Most brewers used a mix of Scottish and English barley, depending on price and quality in any one year. And hops from East Kent were widely recognised as the best.

But he ignored his local newspaper's advice to keep down the strength of his beer. Robert Chambers, in his *Traditions of Edinburgh*, recorded Younger's Edinburgh Ale as being: 'a potent fluid, which almost glued the lips of the drinker together and of which few therefore could despatch more than a bottle.' The description was provided by a regular at John Dowie's, a tavern in Liberton's Wynd which was an early stockist. John Dowie, Chambers wrote, 'always brought in the liquor himself (and) decanted it carefully. . .' The price was 3*d.* a bottle for Archibald's strongest ale and 2¼*d.* for the second strength. One of Dowie's customers was Robert Burns, who arrived in Edinburgh in 1786.

That same year, Archibald Younger acquired a second, larger brewery in Croft-an-Righ, an old lane behind the Palace of Holyrood, to the east of the Abbey. Seven years later, in 1793, in partnership with John Sommervail, who later married one of his sisters, he had opened a brand-new brewery at the north back of Canongate, on what is now part of Waverley railway station. With two malt floors, each one hundred feet long, a copious well and ten 30-barrel tuns, it was a large-scale operation by the standards of Edinburgh. Archibald's youngest brother, William II,

VOL. LIX.   THE   No. 3057

EDINBURGH ADVERTISER.

From F R I D A Y April 12, to T U E S D A Y April 16, 1793.

LEITH ALE, PORTER AND TABLE BEER.

WILLIAM YOUNGER, brewer in Leith, most respect-fully acquaints the public, that next month he will open Vaults in Blair Street, for retailing in dozens ALE, PORTER, and TABLE BEER brewed by himself, of a very superior QUALITY and FLAVOUR. The prices will be mentioned in a future advertisement.

Leith, 12th April, 1793.

began selling ale and porter from vaults in Blair Street, Leith, at the same time. Another brother, Richard, was brewing on a small scale in Gentle's Close, off Canongate.

It was a difficult year. The outbreak of war with revolutionary France shattered confidence in the pyramid of notes and bills of exchange which had built up on the assumption that all this paper was convertible, on demand, into gold. Suddenly nervous customers were testing this belief to destruction by asking for their deposits to be paid out in gold. A bank in Newcastle was the first to close its doors; dozens more collapsed as the panic spread. The Bank of England made a big issue of Exchequer bills, which saved over 200 private banks from going under, but its own gold reserves fell from £13m. to only £2.5m. Rumours of a French invasion at Christmas 1796, were the final straw. The price of government securities crashed the following February, after Newcastle farmers once again closed their local bank by demanding gold for their outstanding credit notes, and the Bank of England was forced to stop payment. For the first time the United Kingdom was off the gold standard, a situation which lasted for a quarter of a century.

Among the beleaguered Newcastle businessmen was a 51-year-old brewer named John Barras. Like William Younger, Barras came from a farming family, in his case in Whickham, on the south bank of the Tyne. He had been under 30 when he had begun brewing in partnership with William Johnston of Gateshead in the early 1770s. Twenty-five years later the partners struggled, along with everyone else, to cope during the financial crisis. Banking was an integral part of beer-making. At harvest time, brewers' books would be deeply in the red, as they bought barley and hops. When the new beer went on sale, their cash flow swung the other way, although much of their credit balance was usually tied up in loans to publicans. War with France hit brewers a double blow. The price of wheat and barley leaped, from 43s. a quarter in 1793 to a peak of 126s. a quarter in 1812, and then the financial markets fell apart. Barras came through the crisis, but in 1799 he was advertising for a new partner in his 'well-accustomed brewery and malting business'. Probably Johnston had decided to retire, but he might have been forced to retrench.

Scottish brewers like the Youngers were not so badly affected. The Scots were far more comfortable with paper money than the English and there was nothing like the rush to hoard gold. And not nearly so much money was on loan to publicans. Grizel's retirement in 1794 was almost certainly influenced more by the fact that she had reached 65 than any financial pressure. Alexander Anderson had died in 1781, but she had run his brewery in her own name for another 12 years; she probably underwrote her youngest son's new business and may well have invested in Archibald's latest venture. Both did well. Three years later William II had opened his own Edinburgh brewery, again in the Abbey's precincts, while Archibald was well on the way to a fortune.

SCOTTISH & NEWCASTLE PUBS TODAY

Ye Olde King's Head, Chigwell, on the borders of Epping Forest, was the model for the Maypole Inn in Dickens's *Barnaby Rudge*, and probably dates back to the late 16th century. *Inset*: the pub today.

2

October Ale is Preferred

One of the advantages of strong ale was that it kept for much longer than less alcoholic beer. This also meant it would travel. On 19 May 1802, Thomas Wilson put an advertisement in the *Morning Post Advertiser* announcing that he had just delivered a cargo of Mr William Younger's 'much admired' ale to the Edinburgh Ale Vaults in London in casks and bottles, 'which, being carefully selected by himself from the stock of that famous brewer, will be found on trial to surpass in strength and flavour any ever offered to sale in London.'

There is no evidence that this was the first consignment of Younger's beer to reach the UK's capital, but it might have been. Total exports of Scottish beer to England at the beginning of the 19th century were minute; only 2,000 barrels in 1800. Two years later they were up by 50 per cent, but still almost invisible compared to the output of the smallest of the great London breweries, which produced 'only' 65,000 barrels that year. Scottish strong ale had an even tinier share of the market; William II could have supplied all the 363 1/4 barrels sold to England in 1802. It is safe to say that Younger's Scotch ale was a minority taste in the metropolis, even though Robert Forsyth, the author of *The Beauties of Scotland*, described it as: 'transparent as sherry, without froth or sediment, and of such a moderate degree of astringency or bitterness as to be universally acceptable.'

The majority of Londoners drank porter. This was a dark, heavy, slightly bitter beer which had revolutionised the economics of brewing since the 1740s. Matured in huge butts, it had the twin advantages of converting all the sugar in well-roasted malt into alcohol and of keeping for much longer

The Fleece Inn in the late 19th century.

Ye Olde Fleece Inn, Kendal, Cumbria started life as a coaching inn and brewhouse called the Golden Fleece in 1654.

Edinburgh in 1821, seen from the Glasgow Road, engraved from a painting by Alexander Nasmyth.

The old Edinburgh Excise Office, closed in 1829.

than lighter beer. The larger the container, the more complete the fermentation and the more 'entire' the use of the raw materials. The result was a long-lasting beer which could be made in bulk and sold for 3*d*. a quart – 25 per cent less than its nearest rival. By the end of the 18th century, the 12 largest London brewers were making 1.2m. barrels of porter a year, with the biggest, Barclay Perkins, producing 250,000 barrels.

It is not surprising that William Younger was tempted to make porter himself. He persuaded his bachelor brother Archibald to join him and they hired a London brewer of 'great professional ability' to make porter that would 'vie in every respect with the best that can be imported from London'. The first batch was advertised in the *Edinburgh Evening Courant* in November 1806, at £3 6*s*. per hogshead for the very best quality, £2 16*s*. for the second best and £2 6*s*. for the third quality. The experiment was a failure. The English-style beer was too bitter for Scottish palates and in August 1808, the 'copartnery' of A. C. and W. Younger was dissolved by mutual consent, with William paying off its debts.

The younger brother could afford it. In 1803 he had bought James Blair's Abbey Brewery, which he had redeveloped so successfully that within two years he was able to afford a country house with 600 acres at Beattock, in Dumfriesshire. He found the time to enjoy his new estate in large part because he could rely on the skills and industry of Alexander Smith, his 'superintendent' at the brewery. William made Smith a partner in 1811. Seven years later, following the death of another partner, Robert Hunter,

Smith's share of the business was increased to 25 per cent in a new copartnery agreement running until 1836, when William would be coming up to 70.

Archibald had done even better. He had a substantial share portfolio and owned a string of houses and shops in Edinburgh, as well as farmland on the city's outskirts. He had been experimenting with ways of making waste ground more fertile for more than a decade, planting vegetables with deep roots and then ploughing them under as manure, and trying to grow barley in sand. The year after his partnership with William II ended, Archibald bought 16,000 acres near Dunoon, Argyllshire, and effectively retired from brewing. He spent ten absorbed years on his estate, leaving the management of his brewery to a new partner, Thomas Cadell, although he kept an eye on its performance. This flourished in spite of doubled excise duty to help pay for the war with France and, until 1812, the United States, and positively boomed until Napoleon was finally defeated at Waterloo in 1815. The end of the war caused an industrial recession. In 1817, Edinburgh Council put 1,600 registered unemployed to work building roads; thousands of unregistered begged or stole. Sales of strong ale fell by 13 per cent for two years, but recovered in 1819.

That year Archibald Younger died, aged 62. He left everything to William II, as Richard had died in 1806. William sold his brother's Canongate brewery and two years later disposed of the Dunoon estate for £22,000. In 1821, Grizel also died, aged 90, leaving her sole surviving son another inheritance. For the first time for a generation, all the family's brewing interests were under the one name, William Younger & Company.

William II grasped the opportunity to become Edinburgh's premier brewer. In 1825 he bought an old town house in the Canongate, once the home of the Marquess of Lothian, named the Lothian Hut. Four years later he leased an adjoining property with a 70-ft frontage, with an option to buy the freehold in ten years' time, which gave him a further small brewery, a malt loft, a coach house, a kiln, offices, houses and a well.

In 1836, William II began to prepare for retirement by making his elder son a partner, along with Alexander Smith's son, Andrew. Aged 35, William III was a married man who had already fathered two sons, William IV and Henry, so he had done his duty in terms of perpetuating the family name. A victim of ill-health, his main interest was the family estate and he had no intention of becoming a brewer. It was a familiar predicament.

Fortunately, Andrew filled the breach. He had begun his apprenticeship in the brewery at the age of 16 and at 23 he was a master of the trade. Perhaps even more importantly, he was dedicated to improving what was still an art, as the notes he kept for his own sons revealed:

'Barley: when barley is moderate in price, buy as much in spring and summer of new thrashed barley and kiln dry it. It will last you for malting between September and November. Even if later prices are moderate, we

French Cuirassiers in combat with Highlanders and Scots Greys at the Battle of Waterloo (Matthew Dubourg, 1816).

The Tolbooth and High Street in Canongate. Archibald Younger set up his own brewery on the North Back of Canongate near by.

Early 19th-century beer delivery.

The contract of copartnery between
William II Younger and Alexander Smith.

always found that barley managed this way malted uncommonly well. You may occasionally make good malt in May, but it depends entirely on the weather. Be most particular about the malt being well and thoroughly dried. Your ale will never be fine nor keep unless made from well-dried malt kept in bins from the air.

'Curing Tuns: dissolve gum shellac in alcohol and give tubs three coats. Be careful that fire does not come in contact with it before it dries, as it is inflammable. German brewers use a scrubbing brush and sand to clean all their wooden utensils. Also when they use sugar they put in potato sugar instead of cane sugar, as they find it has less acidity.

'Keeping Ales: whenever you commence making keeping ales, upon looking at the cookers you will see an oily substance floating on the top of the worts. That is the oil of the hops. At first I paid it no attention, till one night after the worts were run to the tun, I saw the bottom of the cooker was covered with this substance, which I considered was very detrimental to the keeping quality of the ale. So every night before the worts are slacked, make a man go round with an old turning scoop and break in all the oily matter by throwing the worts over the cooker.

'Racking Ale: racking should be avoided as much as possible. We were very short of hops for our Glasgow business one June to complete their orders. To save the expense of new casks, we filled old ones and racked into them as they came to hand, with a good quantity of finings. We found afterwards we had better have bought new, as a good many were returned. They never fined well and were flat in bottle.'

Andrew Smith's empirical approach was a measure of how ignorant the industry still was about the chemical processes that were involved in manufacturing beer. The author of *The Scottish Ale-Brewer*, W. H. Roberts, might claim in 1837 that since the introduction of Allan's Saccharometer, which measured the specific gravity of beer, 'the art of brewing has ceased to be a mere mechanical operation, which may be conducted by any illiterate person . . . and has attained the rank of a science.' But this was a long way from the truth, which was that beer making was still, in essence, a 'mystery'.

Andrew's skills were soon put to the test. Younger's beers were going through a bad patch. There were many complaints about its bottled ale being cloudy and flat. The firm's new managing partner at first thought that the problem was caused by the employees not being particular enough at cleansing. 'If it came to a very light frothy head in the cask,' he noted, 'I thought it would fine more. Afterwards I was satisfied that

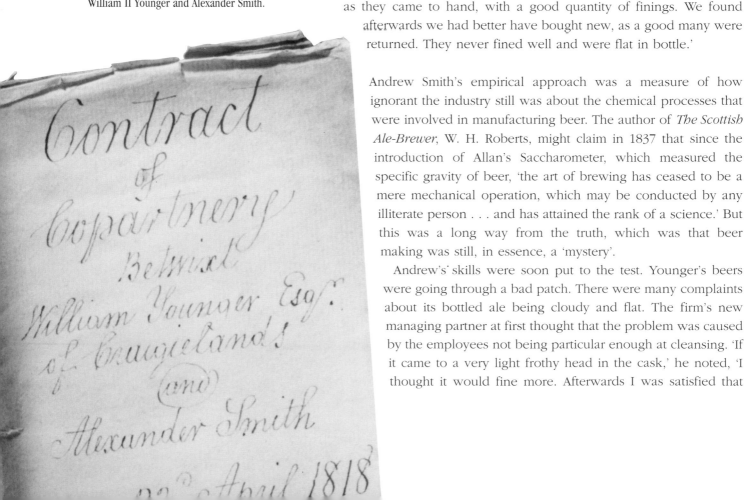

Contract
of
Copartnery
Betwixt
William Younger Esqr.
of Craigieland's
(and)
Alexander Smith
. . . April 1818

Greenock, on the west coast of Scotland, from which beer was exported to the Americas.

the reverse was the case. In September 1837, I commenced cleansing to come to a large head in the cask. Generally if it was beat at 10 p.m. it was cleansed next afternoon in mild weather. During cold or frosty weather, it was cleansed sooner. Be most particular in cleansing to come to a large head in the cask.'

He also quickly learned that it was a mistake to make the ale too pale. 'Whenever barley is dear, the ale (particularly the 60/-, 80/- and 100/-) should be made a good bold colour. More attention is paid to colour in a dear year as the customers know the ale must be weaker then and if pale they cry out at once – especially the country dealers.'

A year later he faced another problem. 'In the beginning of the season we had a large demand. Consequently the ale was sent out a day or two after it was cleansed and the dealers being generally in immediate want got very impatient for bottling it and kept looking at it every week which flattened some of it so much that it never fined with them. We brought it away after standing six or eight weeks. We put it on the gauntries without venting and in three days it became as fine as wine. We therefore determined to keep a much larger stock and upon no account to send ale out until it had at least been 14 days in the cask. It fined with us very soon and with the dealer it was generally fine in ten days.'

But in 1839 he confessed that the real mistake lay in not boiling fast enough. 'The wort coppers were the old construction, with a strong draught up the chimney without a check. I made the bricklayer build a bridge at the mouth of the flue to contract the draught and bring the heat more to the bottom. It acted as a bellows and boiled the hops most furiously. From that day we had no complaints as to fining even when it was bottled only eight

Small brewhouse, 1820s.

Bull and Last in Kentish Town, 1820, one of London's many coaching inns.

'The Gin Shop' by George Cruikshank, 1829. The inscription at the base of the picture reads, 'now Oh dear, how shocking the thought is / They make the gin from aquafortis: / They do it on purpose folks lives to shorten / And tickets it up at two pence a quartern.'

or ten days after coming off the tun – and we found it was better not to keep above a week's supply on hand.'

In spite of these problems, Younger's ales and beers were selling well. The company's order books listed customers throughout Scotland, reaching as far as the Shetlands and the Orkneys. The north-east of England had also become an important market, with particularly strong demand from Darlington, Gateshead, Newcastle, Scarborough and Sunderland. And Younger's London agent was regularly ordering up to 900 barrels a month – a very profitable business, as strong Scotch ale was a premium product in the capital, selling for 8s. 5d. a bottle, the same price as Burton ale, 1s. 5d. more than Guinness's popular Irish stout and nearly twice the cost of a quart of porter.

The reason for the rise in sales was partly growth in the population, although this was more true of England, where numbers doubled in the first half of the 19th century. Scotland's population, although rising, was held down by emigration, part of it caused by land clearances, and low life expectancy. Lord Grey's Reform Act of 1832, sparked by a rising of farm labourers following revolution in Paris two years earlier, had yet to have an impact on public health in Scotland. Indeed, it had coincided with an epidemic of cholera, which had been working its way up from London, where it first struck in the UK, for the past two years. But the Reverend Thomas Guthrie, who became minister of the Greyfriars Kirk in Edinburgh, thought it was not disease or death that was the worst. 'It was the starvation, the drunkenness, the rags, the heartless, hopeless miserable condition of the people – the debauched and drunken mothers, the sallow, yellow, emaciated children – their wants, both temporal and spiritual, which one felt themselves unable to relieve – that sometimes overwhelmed me.'

Excessive drinking was a national problem. Ever since the Government had reduced duty on spirits to 7s. a gallon in 1825, consumption of gin in England and whisky in Scotland had grown hugely. English breweries had also been adversely affected by what was known as the Duke of Wellington's Beer House Act, passed in 1830, which allowed any householder liable for the Poor Rate to sell beer from his home or shop on payment of two guineas a year. This had not had much impact on Scottish brewers, most of whom owned few public houses of their own and were happy to sell to anyone. But the growing strength of the Temperance movement was a matter of concern.

In 1833, a Select Committee sat to inquire into the extent, causes and consequences of the 'Prevailing Vice of Intoxication among the Labouring Classes of the United Kingdom'. It found the immediate cause to be the increase in the number of places where alcoholic drink was sold, which was up to an average of one for every 20 families. The consequences to the individual were: 'the destruction of health and mental capacity and vigour; the irritation of worst passions, and the extinction of moral and religious principles.' And the impact on the national welfare included: 'the waste of grain by conversion of nutritious food into poison; loss of productive labour, averaging one day in six; retardation of improvement; increase of pauperism; spread of crime.' The Committee suggested a score of changes, including annual licensing by magistrates and restricted opening on Sundays, neither of which appealed to publicans. Again, however, Younger's was relatively unaffected, as the attack was not aimed at beer, which was still seen as a healthy and relatively harmless beverage.

But Scotland could not completely escape the effects of the recession which followed bad harvests throughout the British Isles in 1838, although it was nothing like as badly hit as the cotton mills of Manchester and Bolton, the kilns of the Potteries, the ironworks and collieries of the Black Country, and the cloth towns in the west of England.

One answer was to find new markets. Younger's had been exporting small quantities of strong ale to Scottish emigrants in the Americas for a long time, as had other Scottish brewers. But the

Holyrood Palace gate, c.1815.

Drawing of a beerhouse by Thomas Rowlandson, c.1800. The popular view was that gin drinkers were intemperate; beer drinkers were wholesome.

Making ready for a delivery: the dray waits outside.

The arrival of the railway in Edinburgh: the North British Railway seen from the North Bridge in 1846, four years after the opening of Waverley station.

trade had seldom climbed over 4,000 barrels a year. In 1840, however, the country's overseas sales jumped to 16,000 barrels. Within a few years, Younger's was exporting to most of the British colonies in Africa, Asia and Australasia, as well as increasing its trade with the USA and central and southern America, especially the West Indies. One factor behind the sudden increase was an improvement in passage times.

In April 1838, within 24 hours of each other, the *Sirius* and the *Great Western* completed the first crossings of the Atlantic under steam. Their achievement was only a symbol of things to come, as it would be many years before steam supplanted sail for most of the world's cargoes. But the Industrial Revolution was having an impact on sailing ships as well. Wire rope and shrouds were improving their ability to point into the wind and mechanical winches were transforming sail handling. Steel tubes were even beginning to be used for masts and spars. Nothing could combat the vagaries of the wind, of course, and the fastest tea and wool clippers only averaged about 6 knots. But that was appreciably better than before. And the arrival of steam tugs dramatically reduced the time spent manoeuvring in and out of port.

Even so, voyages to Australasia and the Far East took a very long time. 'Ale should arrive during the open season from September to April,' warned Younger's Bombay agent in 1845. 'October ale is preferred, but it would require to be shipped promptly to arrive in April.' He knew what he was talking about. Fifty thousand gallons of British beer which had arrived that July had been so bad, it had been poured into the harbour. Exporting to the USA was quicker, where, as the firm's New York agent reported cheerfully in 1848: 'the sale of Scotch ale is increasing with us every year.'

Younger's English business was also poised to benefit from another revolution in transport. In 1842, Waverley station was opened. The railway had arrived in Edinburgh. The Younger and Smith families both invested enthusiastically in railway shares, as well as ensuring that their beer

was stocked by the grand hotels that sprang up to accommodate the flood of travellers. Again, the immediate effect on the firm's business was small. Most of its beer continued to be delivered on horse-drawn drays. But rail transport costs were a fifth of those by wagon. Although bulk cargoes by sea remained competitive in price for a long time, the coastal trade could not match its new rival for speed.

When William III and Alexander Smith died, they left their shares in the brewing firm to their sons William IV and Andrew. In 1849, the centenary of its notional formation by his great-grandfather, William IV's stake in the business was shown in the accounts as £22,736 7*s.* 0*d.*, while Andrew's was put at £11,830 13*s.* 1*d.* That valued Younger's business at approximately £2m. in today's money.

In April 1838, the *Great Western* completed one of the first crossings of the Atlantic under steam. The firm's New York agent reported cheerfully in 1848: 'The sale of Scotch ale is increasing with us every year.'

The Two Brewers, overlooking Chipperfield Common in Hertfordshire, dates back to the 18th century. The pub acquired a certain fame as training quarters for many great prize fighters such as Jem Mace and Bob Fitzsimmons, who would spar in the Club Room and take their runs round the Common. Cricket on the Common has also been a source of much custom over the years.

3

William McEwan, who founded the
Fountainbridge Brewery in 1856.

The Quality will be Good

William McEwan received the letter from the Union Bank of Scotland offering to 'feu' him a 14,000 sq. ft plot of land in Fountain Bridge, Edinburgh, at a ground rent of £40 per annum 'for the erection of a brewery' on 2 October 1856. He accepted immediately.

McEwan had been looking for a brewery of his own for at least two years. His father had been a shipowner in Alloa, at the head of the Firth of Forth, and McEwan had gone to Alloa Academy and then worked as a clerk for the Alloa Coal Company, in a wool merchant's office in Glasgow, and as a bookkeeper in a Yorkshire spinning mill, before joining the Heriot Brewery in Edinburgh's Grassmarket in November 1851. The Heriot Brewery belonged to his uncles John and David Jeffrey. Five years later, aged 29, William McEwan was ready to go it alone, equipped with a rare combination of administration, accountancy and risk management skills, as well as a sound practical knowledge of brewing.

There had been no secret about his ambition to set up on his own. James Younger, the heir to the George Younger Brewery in Alloa, who had married McEwan's sister Janet in 1850, had investigated the attractions of several breweries in Liverpool on his behalf in 1854. William's youngest brother John had also been involved in the search for a suitable existing business to buy. One had proved impossible to find. The decision to start from scratch, though, was a brave move, for the family as well as McEwan, as his mother and another uncle were backing him with £500 loans, with a further £1,000 borrowed from the bank.

But William McEwan was sublimely confident. By the time the Union

Early photograph of the
Fountainbridge Brewery,
Edinburgh, constructed by
William McEwan in 1856.

Waiting for opening time on
Sunday, London, 1856.

Bank's letter arrived, he was already driving ahead with the construction of the Fountainbridge Brewery. A stream of letters chivvied suppliers, accepted tenders, confirmed bondsmen for future malt duty, arranged water supplies to 'my malt barn in Himlus close, off the Grassmarket, with a malting capacity of twelve quarters every week', and agreed insurance cover of £900 for his new premises, plus another £500 for machinery and utensils, and a further £400 on three old houses on the site, for which he had paid the Union Bank £260. He also insured his malt barn, although not before querying the terms of the policy issued by the British Linen Co. 'I should like an explanation of the following clause, viz: "The company will not be liable for stock on the kiln burnt or damaged by the process of kiln drying." It is only in the process of kiln drying that any danger of fire occurs in the malt barn. If I am not protected by the policy from this risk, it will be of very little use insuring.'

He was a demanding client. 'I have your estimate for building the furnaces and flues on my premises at Fountain Bridge,' he wrote to Robert Bruce, who was making them to order in Union St. 'From the longeness (*sic*) of the sum named, I am inclined to think that you must have made some mistake.' But he was obviously committed to Bruce, as he continued: 'I wish the flues of the wort copper to admit of a small quantity of liquor being boiled without detriment to the copper. I do not think the flues should be carried higher than 20 inches.' He finished: 'I expect the boiler makers will be on the ground in the beginning of next week, and we shall be in great confusion if the furnace is not built by then.'

Confusion, though, was inevitable. 'I have your favour of 30 ult,' he wrote tersely to the boilermaker. 'There was certainly more delay in putting the boiler into position than I expected, but this was in great measure caused by circumstances which you could have obviated. In the first place the boiler seems to have been forwarded without giving the railway company special instructions about prompt delivery, and in consequence it did not arrive till late on Tuesday. And another cause of delay was your having rivetted on the cover, which had to be lifted off before the boiler could be got in at the door. In these circumstances, I can only allow you one half the amount paid your men.'

And inevitably the plumbers came under the whip. 'I must urge upon you the necessity of getting in the pipes for the water pump without another day's delay. We can neither get the pavement under the mash house laid nor the close raised to the required level until you do. Pray use your utmost exertions to push on this matter.'

They obviously did as they were told, as William McEwan brewed his first beer before the end of December, in spite of a severe storm which stopped outdoor work for a week. By then he had appointed Robert Brown as his Glasgow agent on the recommendation of James Younger, although not before some hard bargaining in which Brown had managed to increase his commission from 7.5 per cent to 8.5 per cent. He immediately demonstrated his worth, however, with a flood of orders which McEwan was at first hard pressed to meet. Other agents signed up, such as David Stocks & Co. of Leith, who accepted responsibility for sales north of the Firth of Forth (at 7.5 per cent).

Not surprisingly, McEwan's first beers were strongly influenced by those being produced by the Heriot Brewery and by George Younger & Co. in Alloa, which was one of the earliest producers of 'India' pale ale. This was a clear, refreshing beer, highly impregnated with the finest hops, which had proved extremely popular in hot countries. Although initially brewed in London, it was Scottish and Burton brewers who realised its potential in colonial markets. The first shipments, incidentally, went to Scottish émigrés in the West Indies; only later did it arrive in the Indian subcontinent. India pale ale was a 'strengthening, exhilarating and wholesome beverage'. But it obviously had to have a long life and travel well, qualities that many brewers found hard to achieve.

McEwan, though, had the benefit of the latest technology, such as William Steel's patent mashing machine, for which he paid a royalty of £8 8s. 6d. at the beginning of January 1857. Invented four years earlier, this was a cylinder with internal rotating vanes to mix up hot water and ground malt before they flowed into the mash tun. It saved time, labour and raw materials, and brewers were rushing to buy it. Not that Steel's machine was perfect from the word go. Andrew Smith, who had bought one for Younger's the previous year, found the ground malt fell into the centre of the hopper and formed large lumps in the mash tun. Smith cured this by putting a wood block shaped something like a horse's saddle about two feet under the feeder to distribute the meal and husks more evenly. Two years later, he improved the process even more by drilling additional holes in the false bottom of the mash tun, to allow freer passage of the liquor.

McEwan's first beer was ready for delivery by the middle of January 1857. ('So far everything

A barmaid 'pulling' pints in 1849. Bar pumps began to be installed in pubs in the first half of the 19th century.

'Flooring' the barley as part of the malting process in the early 1850s.

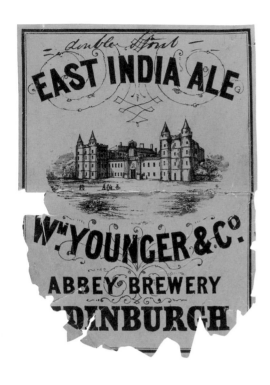

The *Flying Cloud*. Younger's beer was first carried to Australia and other overseas destinations in clipper ships such as this.

has gone favourably and I incline to think the quality will be good,' he told Brown.) He began with lower-strength ale, which sold for four or five guineas a hogshead, but was soon producing seven, eight and even ten guinea ales. And in April Brown asked him if he could meet an export order from a Mr Clelland in Australia. McEwan replied confidently that he had in his time made a great deal of pale ale for the Australasian market.

Demand in Australia had risen enormously since the discovery of gold at Ballarat in the state of Victoria and Bathurst in New South Wales. Four hundred thousand hopeful prospectors had emigrated from Britain in almost as large a gold rush as the one in California at much the same time. Several Scottish breweries had capitalised on the diggers' thirst, including Younger's.

William III's middle son Henry went too, but not to sell beer. He had joined the family firm in 1852, aged 20, after studying at the Royal College for Civil Engineers in Putney, but three years later he left to work on a sheep and cattle station next to the Murray river in Victoria. He stayed for five years, and letters suggest that he invested in the station and dabbled in gold prospecting. There is no hint that he acted as an agent for Younger's beer, perhaps fortunately, as he would probably have upset the company's existing importers. By the mid-1850s, Younger's had a world-wide network of agents, stretching from Auckland to Valparaiso, although it was still strongest in the Americas.

Exporting was a tough business. Consignments arriving 'only fit for vinegar', broken bottles, 'passing off' by competitors who copied Younger's labels, slow voyages, shipwrecks, lost cargoes – forty casks once lay for two years in Tobago before being sold. Amazingly, that beer was still in good

condition, although it had become a little too strong for local taste. Ironically, the importer's storeroom was burned down a few months later and all his stock was lost. But most of the company's beer arrived in reasonable condition and it usually found eager customers. 'Your mark is well known,' wrote a Cuban buyer, 'and I can get through 100 barrels every fourteen days.' 'We could have sold readily 500 casks of your beer,' reported a Boston importer. 'We regret that you are discouraged by results of consignments,' a Chilean agent apologised. 'We have since sold many lots and can run off some thousands of casks a year to our numerous customers . . . We like your beer.'

The British army liked it, too. Younger's was one of the suppliers of beer for the troops sent to the Crimea in 1854 to defend Turkey against what was described as Russian aggression, and garrisons throughout the Empire were beginning to order consignments, although competition was stiff from George Younger, Tennents of Glasgow, and Burton breweries like Allsopp and Bass.

The business was also fairly small scale. Scotland's direct beer exports totalled just over 30,000 barrels in 1855 and, even after adding in the casks shipped via London, overseas trade was probably no more than 10 per cent of the country's total output, which had risen to 500,000 barrels

The Charge of the Light Brigade, 1855. British troops in the Crimea were supplied with beer by Younger's.

Label from a bottle of Younger's ale, which was part of a consignment supplied to the Crimea.

John Barras jnr, painted c.1824. The business he inherited from his father would in due course become Newcastle Breweries.

The railway viaduct built across part of Barras's land in 1838. Its brick arches provided new cellars for the Tyne Brewery.

by the middle of the century. Admittedly the trend was upwards, but the home market was much more important. Thanks to Brown, more than half McEwan's £40,000 turnover in 1860 was in Glasgow and the colliery, iron and cotton towns of Ayrshire, Lanarkshire and Renfrewshire, with Edinburgh in second place, and perhaps 20 per cent split between north and east Scotland and Tyneside.

Newcastle brewed a surprisingly small proportion of the beer drunk in the city and its satellite on the south bank of the Tyne, Gateshead; perhaps no more than a third. One reason was the 'indifferent' water used to make the local brew, which was a very sweet dark ale with a sub-acid flavour called Newcastle mild. With tastes changing in favour of paler ales, local brewers like John Barras had found it hard to compete with leading brands from Edinburgh and Burton-on-Trent. But that did not mean they were all doing badly.

Barras was still thriving. John Barras had died in 1811, worth £30,000 (equal to nearly £2m. today), but his son John jnr had continued to develop the business, as well as diversifying into wine and spirits. By 1824, Barras was producing more than 40,000 barrels a year, of which about two-thirds was strong 'old' beer, and output continued to grow. By 1838, the Gateshead brewery had become an extensive complex, with six houses, three open yards, the brewhouse, corn lofts, maltings and kilns, spirit cellars, storehouses and other outbuildings filling a large area between the town's High Street and West Street. The railway arrived in the

city that year and a viaduct was built across part of Barras's land; as well as £3,000 in compensation, the viaduct's brick arches provided the brewery with new cellars.

By then, too, Barras had acquired several local pubs. More were added in the 1840s, at the end of which Newcastle was reckoned to be as well provided with public houses as any town or city in the United Kingdom. In 1848, with two of his sons, Henry and George, on the Grand Tour of Europe, his eldest, John III, born a deaf mute and a fourth mentally handicapped, John jnr took his sister's son, Charles Reed, into the firm. It was a prophetic decision. Three years later Henry and George both died of typhoid in Milan, leaving Charles Reed as John jnr's *de facto* successor in the brewery. Reed proved a more than adequate lieutenant, and by the end of the 1850s the Barras brewery was one of the largest on the Tyne. But, like its rivals, it remained overshadowed by imports. Younger's alone sold 25 per cent of its beer in the north-east of England, much of it through Reid Brothers, a Newcastle brewery founded in 1837.

Another 20 per cent of Younger's beer went to London, some of it on the way to the colonies, but much for immediate consumption. The efforts of Andrew Smith and the company's new head brewer, Andrew Thomson, had made Younger's Scotch ale ever more popular in the UK's capital. In spite of 28 years' experience, Smith was still experimenting. Since Sir Robert Peel repealed the Corn Laws in 1846 (introduced by Lord Liverpool's government at the end of the Napoleonic war, the law was a blatant piece of protectionism for British landowners, imposing heavy duties on foreign imports if the price of UK corn fell below a certain point) most Scottish brewers had been importing barley from the Continent, as well as the Middle East and North America. Smith had been particularly impressed by the 1856 crop he bought from Silesia. That year, too, Younger's had begun purchasing hops from Sussex and Suffolk, as well as East Kent, 'being tempted by their quality and price', and in 1857 the company started buying Worcester hops for the beginning of the season, as they were milder. Smith always asked for bulk samples from London, which he weighed carefully. 'Mistakes have sometimes been made as to weight under suspicious circumstances,' he noted wryly.

Younger's had begun bottling for export in 1843, but did not do much until 1856. At first there were a great number of breakages, owing to inexperience in handling and bottling too soon. The company found it could not bottle pale ales for warm climates until they had been kept nearly twelve months in cask. Even strong ales needed to mature for several months before bottling. Any earlier and the results could be literally explosive.

The repeal of the Corn Laws enabled brewers to buy barley at reasonable prices from abroad.

Andrew Smith, Younger's partner, with his son, Andy and wife, Jessie, c.1860.

Passing on the craft to the next generation. Pages from 'Notes on Brewing for my sons Alexander and Andrew Smith 25 Nov 1858'.

Smith was not the only Edinburgh brewer to be unhappy about the quality of Scottish malt. 'At the brewers' dinner in 1859, a few remained to an oyster and had a long talk about malting. The general opinion was that we were all right in the brewing department, but all wrong in the malting. Mr McEwan, who had been in a good few English maltings, said we were sadly behind on wages – they paid their men 22*s.* a week – and that the English workman when he had young floors was never more than six or seven hours out of his barn, and always kept the malt growing.'

Smith had a particular problem. That March, Younger's had bought yet another of its local rivals. Alexander Berwick's brewery stood on a spacious plot off Gentle's Close, where Richard Younger had made beer. Berwick, indeed, had bought Richard's business at the beginning of the century and had built up a flourishing trade, but since his death in 1855, his nephews had allowed the business to slip through their fingers, losing £15,000 in three years. Younger's only paid £1,600 for the brewery, plus a four-year lease on its yard and cellars.

A dog show held at the Queen's Tavern, Haymarket, London, 1855.

The motive behind the acquisition was to boost exports, as Berwick's beers were reportedly highly regarded for keeping well in both San Francisco and Melbourne. The brewery's local trade was small, owing to its inability to make a sweet enough ale to suit Edinburgh tastes. The reason, apparently, was the quality of its water. Smith was not convinced. After a year's experience of Berwick's maltings, he decided that it was bad ventilation of the kilns which prevented the brewery making sweet ale – 'they were quite choked up for want of air below and the ventilators on the roof were too small. We increased them largely both above and below, which improved the malt wonderfully.' It was a pleasing triumph.

Newcastle was becoming a thriving industrial city when J. M. Turner painted this scene in the early 19th century.

Export label bound for Demerara in British Guiana, South America.

4

A Most Vicious Principle

Henry Younger returned home from Australia in 1861, not noticeably sadder or wiser than when he had left five years earlier. But he was definitely poorer, as his attempt to extract money from the trustees of his father's estate revealed. He argued bitterly with his elder brother William that he was surely entitled to dip into his legacy to buy straight into the family business. It took him some time to accept that the trustees were not connected with the company and it was out of their power to pay for a partnership. His only choice was to build up a stake in the business out of his earnings as an employee, in the same way as his younger brother David and Andrew Smith's son Alexander were doing.

It was even difficult to find him a suitable job, after so long an absence. Fortunately, Younger's had recently opened new offices in London, at St Paul's Wharf, Upper Thames Street, where the first manager, Robertson, had not impressed Andrew Smith. Appointing Henry in his place killed two birds with one stone. Nothing loath, the firm's newest partner, albeit one with a paid-up shareholding of only £1,900 compared to William IV's £82,000 and Andrew Smith's £46,000, moved south early in 1862. Henry was not one to let a shortage of cash cramp his style. One of his earliest actions was to order a racy set of wheels in the form of: 'a new Mail Phaeton of the very handsomest description, with Collinge's Patent axles, shafts for one horse and pole and bar for two horses. Patent leather hood to driving seat made to fold very flat down. Painted and lined to your order, and finished altogether in the most complete and handsome manner for the sum of £95 sterling' (say £6,000 today, plus, of course, the horses).

The Bridge Inn, near Norwich. There has been a river
crossing near by for 900 years. The pub used to be a
centre for smuggling, especially gin from Holland.

Younger's opened new offices at St Paul's Wharf, London in the late 1850s.

Andrew Smith quickly made sure that his newest colleague's mind was on his job. 'My dear Younger,' he wrote on 12 April, 'I am sorry you are getting on so slow with the accounts. Are you not adopting the plan of bringing in the collectors in the afternoon, when there are no callers? As Robertson is paying so little attention to the business, I think it desirable that you should commence at once.' And on 1 May, after a swift visit to London, he wrote again: 'My dear Henry, As Robertson has not been in the habit of collecting, it is the less likely he will do so. The only thing I think you should do at once would be to see all the bottlers, as Mr R used to call on them, and let them know you are going to reside in London and will in future collect them. In talking to customers, do not say anything against R. If they ask any questions, you can say that we thought the business would be better attended by a partner being on the spot. It would never do to adopt Carr's idea to put it on the grounds of our business increasing too slowly.' (Carr was one of Younger's salesmen.)

Obviously the London business was in poor shape. But at least it meant that Henry had nowhere to go but up. Evidence that he was putting his nose to the grindstone emerged a year later, when Alex Cuthbert, Younger's secretary, advised him that the net profit available for division between the partners for the year to 30 June 1863 was £29,876 and his share was £5,601. Predictably, Henry had already drawn more than £2,000 in advance, but even so it meant his share capital was up to nearly £8,000.

Henry's success in London swiftly repaired any damage caused to his sensitive ego from having to re-establish his worth to the company, and he was soon giving as good as he got in the stream of correspondence that flowed between the partners. Too soon, perhaps. 'My dear Henry,' his brother David wrote on 4 March 1864. 'Your letter of yesterday to hand. I think we hardly deserve that blowing up about the casks. Perhaps you will remember

A smart mail phaeton, similar to the one ordered by Henry Younger on his return from Australia.

that you gave Paris particular directions to take the numbers of all the bad casks returned from London in order that you might trace them and see where they had been. Now that we do that, you blow us up for it, you snob. Please shut up in future.'

And he was helped by the strength of the UK economy, still in the grips of the boom sparked by the repeal of the Corn Laws and the subsequent adoption of a policy of (relatively) free trade. Ever since the Great Exhibition of 1851, demand for almost everything had increased in leaps and bounds and there seemed no reason why it should ever falter, although the American Civil War, which had begun in 1861, had caused a nasty wobble. In Younger's case, this included the failure of its San Francisco agent and a bad debt of $9,000. But by May 1864, Younger's was doing such extraordinary trade that the only question was whether to refurbish Berwick's brewery, which would involve an outlay of from £1,500 to £2,000 and mean finding additional tunroom and other accommodation for the Abbey Brewery. The answer was yes and the renovated building was renamed Holyrood Brewery, with Andrew Thomson's deputy, 26-year-old George Stenhouse, in charge.

In the meantime, though, Thomson had to warn Henry to be cautious about how many orders he took for the summer months, particularly for pale ale. 'I am doing everything in my power to get up a stock, but I am afraid that we shall be found wanting for your demands.'

Henry, however, was coming to the end of his London stint. He was about to get married and in 1865 he moved back to Edinburgh. He was replaced as manager by Alexander Bruce, a young clerk the same age as Stenhouse, who had joined Younger's straight from Edinburgh High School ten years earlier and had spent most of his time in the London office. A small build and a subservient manner camouflaged an acute business brain and a daunting capacity for hard work.

One of Bruce's first jobs was overseeing a move from St Paul's Wharf to new offices and stores in Lambeth. Next to the Lion brewery in Belvedere Road, the site had a 150-ft waterfront on to the Thames with three wharves, and included twelve 'lofty' arches under Hungerford railway bridge, each with a floor space of 4,000 sq. ft.

Another early task was persuading the local magistrates to transfer the licence of The Holyrood, a public house which Younger's had just added to its small but growing portfolio of tied properties in the City. Bruce informed Henry that the pub had escaped by a hair's breadth: 'with two sheets from the police with information against it for gambling and stolen cheques, etc, which the Bench characterised as of the "very gravest character". They said they had had this house under their consideration very frequently and therefore knew it "too well". They however added that the

David Younger, as a lieutenant in the Royal Artillery in the 1860s.

Early picture of the Abbey Brewery, which continued in use until the 1950s.

Alexander Bruce as a young clerk. He replaced Henry Younger as manager of Younger's London offices in 1865.

'Gallowgate Hoppings'. The hoppings was a fair in Gallowgate, where Newcastle Breweries have been producing beer since 1884. The head offices moved to the site in 1960 and today the brewery occupies 20 acres on one side of Gallowgate, opposite Newcastle United football stadium.

party's position to whom the transfer was to be made was a guarantee that it would be conducted differently. Mr Isaacson the Clerk to the Bench put in a good word for us and turned the tide.'

This was just one of the regular flow of letters to and from Edinburgh, all handwritten with steel-nibbed pens dipped in ink. The first successful transatlantic telegraph cable had been laid between London and New York in 1866, but it would be a quarter of a century before the telephone became widely available. Instead, a continuous and indefatigable correspondence underpinned all Younger's activities, maintaining its links with its agencies and branches and keeping the partners and their senior managers informed about everything concerning their business.

Some were more important than others, of course. An example is the letter from David Younger to his brother Henry on 13 March 1866, from the Abbey Brewery: 'We have had a bad accident here last night. The new tuns were being proved and came down, bringing down two vats of porter and a large portion of the barley loft above them. The cellar was flooded and a great number of casks smashed and emptied. It happened about half past eight in the evening and luckily there was no one near. If it had been in the daytime, it must have killed someone. They are getting it pretty well cleared out, but I expect there is some thousands of pounds of damage done.'

Another was the private advice sent to Bruce by Alex Cuthbert at the end of August that it looked like being a bad season for the company, with all the pale ale in the cellars going sour. 'But we find that bicarbonate of soda has a most wonderful effect. It makes the ale quite sound. We bottled this way and you could not tell it from the finest ale. We hear that the Burton brewers regularly use this article in summer.'

Most letters concerned the trivia which any business has to cope with, such as the query from Younger's Belfast agent, R. J. Irvine, in March 1867, about casks from Edinburgh. 'On the tap side the number is branded between the two words William Younger. On the other side there is a vacant space between and we suppose it is there you wish us to brand the B on the musty casks.'

Or the inconclusive report by PC William Walters on the activities of the drivers of Younger's London van between 2.30 and 7.45 p.m. on 11 February 1868. 'After leaving Blackfriars Rd, they went to their stores in Belvedere Rd and left three empty barrels and one full; from there to Sloane St where they left two small barrels; afterwards went to the Kensington Arms, Warwick Rd, Kensington, there they left three hogsheads; left at 6.15 p.m. with one full barrel, which was brought home by the short man, the tall one leaving him at the Palace stables. They stopped twice in returning but did not bring any empty casks home with them.'

Andrew Smith's letter to Henry Younger on 7 March 1870, however, was one of the more serious. 'Dear Henry, I am very sorry to tell you that the Liverpool affair is a very bad one – in fact a total loss – and I fear our business has been kept together by the most lavish expenditure in every shape. Mitchell says, as far as he can see, there has been no system; everyone helping themselves; and I fear B has been drinking hard and spending a great deal of money foolishly. We have only retained one of his travellers and his brother for office work. B has told Cuthbert and myself no end of big ones.'

The Liverpool loss came at a bad time, as margins in the brewing trade in general were under pressure from high barley prices. But

Dick and Jim, two of the many dray horses at Holyrood Brewery in 1871.

The Custom House, Liverpool, in the late 19th century by Atkinson Grimshaw.

Younger's position in the port was too valuable to abandon, as it was the firm's gateway to Ireland as well as the north-west of England. Instead, the firm decided to invest in new and larger premises. They took two years to build, but on 11 May 1872 Mitchell and Alex Cuthbert entertained 150 Liverpudlian publicans and representatives of the drinks trade to a lavish lunch at Younger's brand-new 'extensive stores and offices' in Brockley Buildings, South John Street. Replying to the toast 'William Younger & Co', William Rothwell made the only reference to the firm's unfortunate recent past in Liverpool when he commented that some time ago his hosts 'could not have mustered such a company as was present if they had given each guest something to visit their table.' But he made amends with some glowing remarks about Mitchell's achievements.

Cuthbert responded with a promotional speech about Younger's. It was, he said, the largest brewer in Edinburgh and business was continuing to expand day-by-day. 'The firm has for long had a hold on Scotland. For 40 years it has had a hold on London. It now has a substantial hold on Liverpool. But its connection is not merely Scotch, English or Irish. It is world-wide. (Cheers).'

A more comprehensive description of the company's assets and business appeared in a supplement to the *Licensed Victuallers' Guardian.* More than a few fulsome words about 'the delectable beverage' produced by Younger's were followed by the information that production at its Abbey and Holyrood breweries was between 3,000 and 5,000 barrels a week, and that a new wing had been added to the maltings in Canonmills which had increased their capacity by 20,000 quarters. The breweries covered 12 acres and were capable of brewing over 60,000 quarters annually. 'The strength and solidity of all the buildings that Messrs. Younger erect are remarkable and no expense seems to be spared in rendering them as complete and perfect as possible.' Visitors were also advised to inspect the large stores for export ales

Export bottling stores, Abbey Brewery, Queen's Park, 1860s.

that had just been built opposite Holyrood Palace 'in the baronial style of architecture'. The supplement revealed that Younger's also owned stores in Aberdeen and Glasgow in Scotland, Bristol, Darlington, Derby, Manchester and Newcastle, as well as London and Liverpool, in England, and Belfast, Cork, Drogheda, Dublin and Limerick in Ireland.

Cuthbert's speech, however, was not finished. He moved on to the trade in general and the iniquity of the legislation that the Home Secretary, the Right

Honourable Henry Bruce, proposed to inflict on it following the 1869 Wine and Beerhouse Act, which had at last restricted unlicensed premises. One effect, naturally, was a rise in the value of existing licences. Although these were renewable annually, in practice they were only withdrawn in cases of proved misconduct and even in these cases, such as The Holyrood, local magistrates usually allowed the goodwill of the business and the lease to be transferred to another publican. Licences, in other words, were effectively in perpetuity.

But suddenly the Home Secretary was suggesting limiting all licences to ten years and allowing ratepayers to restrict the number of pubs in their area by a local veto. The potential damage this could cause to their value was incalculable. Scottish brewers, who owned relatively few pubs, were not nearly so vulnerable as English breweries, which had financial ties with huge numbers. But Younger's, with its small but valuable chain of

Mid-19th century hop pickers, painted by George John Pinwell.

Bottled beer being loaded into railway wagons for despatch around the world.

The impact of the 1863 Sunday Closing Bill, according to *Punch*: 'Well, Betsy, if they won't let us get any refreshment o' Sunday out o' doors we must lay in a stock, and drink at home, like the pious Scotch!'

Alexander Smith, c.1868.

houses in London, was concerned enough to publish a four-page pamphlet titled *Reasons For Compensation and Against Permissivism* in May 1871, in which it argued that the power of vetoing was 'a most dangerous and vicious principle, and if once introduced into legislation will rapidly extend to other measures and become tyrannical in its operation.'

It was signed William Younger & Co., Abbey & Holyrood Breweries, Edinburgh, and Belvedere Road, London, and Alexander Bruce probably contributed to its composition, although the principal author was almost certainly Cuthbert. But Bruce's enthusiasm for the trade's position waned as its attack on the bill intensified, as a letter from him to Henry Younger in April 1873 revealed: 'Caudelet of Manchester, Cleaver of Leicester, Edwards of B'ham, Skinner of Sheffield as representatives of the County trade and the new National League are canvassing the wholesale trade firms for a sort of guarantee Secret Service fund, to be used chiefly at elections and such like occasions. They wish to raise £50,000. Bass & Allsopp have each given £500, Ind Coope £250 and other Burton firms in proportion. The enclosed note will show what they have been doing in London. The deputation propose visiting Scotland, but this they state depends entirely upon what encouragement they are likely to receive from your firm, as they think it will be useless calling upon other houses unless they receive your support. The funds will be chiefly spent in opposing the Permissive tactics.

'They are aware I hold strong views against this Permissive Bill. I doubt the wisdom of war to the knife which some in the trade are disposed to inaugurate. I question the policy of sacrificing political opinion to trade interests and in fact converting trade into a trades union of capital. The question is how far the interests of any class, however powerful, should be made superior to the wishes of the public.

'I have written to Mr Caudelet rather fully, taking care to state very expressly that they are my own individual opinions and in no way reflect the opinions of your house. I cannot advise you whether to follow Messrs Allsopps' footsteps. I think you might ask to defer giving an answer until they inform you what Messrs Truman Hanbury decide.'

Deferential as always, Bruce addressed his superior as 'Dear Sir'. But the courtesy disguised the fact that he had become an important member of Younger's staff, effectively in charge of all its overseas trade and well known throughout the industry at home and abroad. Indeed, he was about to embark on an extended trip to the USA, on which he would chaperone Andrew Smith's elder son, Alexander II, as well as hopefully develop new business in a market where Younger's beers had in recent times acquired an unfortunate reputation for poor quality.

The visit was not a great success. They had only just arrived in New York in September 1873, when one of the USA's largest railway financiers, Jay Cooke, went bust, precipitating a tremendous run on Wall Street and other stock exchanges, 'with every five minutes another house caught up'. Bruce and Smith found their hotel on Fifth Avenue crowded with senators, congressmen and bank presidents, plus President Grant himself, all conferring on what steps to take to contain the crisis. The panic subsided in a few days, but badly affected business, with 'gloom settling down upon everyone'.

Boston was better, with an order for 105 casks of sparkling ale and ten hogsheads of export pale ale. Quebec, Toronto and Ottawa were disappointing, but Chicago 'promises to be the first city in the United States and the great emporium for the West'. Bruce wrote encouragingly to Henry: 'Both Mr Smith and myself can say without the slightest exaggeration that we have not met with a bottle of ale or stout which beats your own brew and we have seen hundreds opened both in the States and Canada. Instead of saying it is hard to beat Bass, I would say it is hard for Bass to beat Wm Youngers. Of course the disasters of past years have to be wiped out and the prejudice in favour of Bass overcome, (but) if the question of capital did not stand in the way I would say develop the export trade as fast as possible.'

However, competition was stiff in San Francisco, Omaha and Salt Lake City. And when the two arrived in St Louis on 1 December, it was to discover that the latest Younger shipment had turned out very badly. The firm's beer was popular in New Orleans, or would have been if there had been any in stock, and Bruce reported that the situation in the southern states was very unsatisfactory. Louisiana was still practically bankrupt eight years after the end of the Civil War, with estates once worth $500,000 being sold for $50,000.

The travellers returned to the UK in time for Christmas, where instead of congratulations, Bruce received a 'blow up' from Henry Younger for suggesting to Alexander Smith that he work in London for a short time, without first asking his employer's permission to do so. Biting his lip, Bruce replied that it was done with the best and purest of motives. 'It would fit him better for going over the Irish ground. It would, I hope, deepen his interest in the home trade, as his visit (to America) has strengthened his interest in exports. I also thought it would enable him more thoroughly to appreciate the policy with reference to the English trade, which you had pursued. As for Mr Alexander altering or interfering with the management of the London trade, no such thought suggested itself to me, far less that it would lead to any alteration in your supervision of it.'

It was the last time that Bruce had to abase himself so deeply.

Wall Street, New York, in the late 19th century. The Wall Street Crash of 1873 had a bad effect on Younger's exports.

A popular vantage point for the Boat Race (on the 1996 race day it took a record £44,000), The Rutland is about halfway along the course near Hammersmith Bridge. The pub, light coloured with balcony and three arched windows, is to the right of the houseboat.

5

At Their Mercy

From Henry Younger's point of view, Alexander Bruce's deference was no more than his due. He had, after all, become the senior partner of Younger's in 1870, when William IV and Andrew Smith decided to retire. Admittedly, they both still owned most of the company's shares, as Henry, his younger brother David and Smith's elder son Alexander, the other partners, could not as yet afford to buy them out. But nominally Henry was in charge.

It was not a particularly good year to take over the management of the brewery, however. The UK was recovering from a recession triggered by the collapse of the Overend Gurney banking group in 1866, but competition in the brewing industry was becoming more intense by the day. In March 1870, Bruce wrote that McEwan's was coming into the London trade and confessed that he would have felt more comfortable if it had been any other Edinburgh brewer. 'When it is considered the rapidity with which his business has grown, it shows that McEwan is terribly in earnest and means to go forward if possible still more.'

Bruce tried to impress on McEwan's new London representative, who had called and presented his card, of the importance of sticking to a 10 per cent discount and not 'going in for cutting up the trade, as two could play at that game'. But his threats had been hollow. Two months later Carr reported that most pale ale brewers were allowing 12.5 per cent discounts, with Jeffreys offering 15 per cent for quick settlement.

Matters worsened the following year, owing to criticisms of Younger's beer. The new season's strong ales responded to being rolled over and Bruce reported that the three brewings he received for export were very fine.

But it had to be recognised that British and overseas tastes were changing in favour of a milder pale ale than Younger's seemed able to produce. As the months passed, complaints about the company's beers mounted. Henry hired a brewer named Black to investigate the problem. After a tour round the breweries and a visit to the hop district in July 1871, Black reported that he was profoundly impressed with the gravity of Younger's position and that the complaints were well founded. The No.2 ale was especially dull-looking and had an 'old' taste. The only compensation was that a good deal of other breweries' London ale was sick.

Problems persisted during the next two years, with the uneven quality of the firm's beer undermining its increasingly desperate efforts to expand its sales. Wages also rose, with Younger's cellarmen asking for an advance in their pay of 2s. a week, plus a further 1s. for everyone who had to work on Sundays cleansing the tuns. 'We need not to attempt to explain the cause of our present petition and therefore we leave it to your consideration, trusting in your wonted liberality we will not be neglected and your memorialists will ever pray.' Twenty-seven men signed the request. Twenty-one were marked as 'good' and given a rise.

By the end of 1873, the business was in real difficulty and the old partners were becoming seriously worried. They made little secret of their dissatis-faction and David Younger told Henry that Andrew Smith was asking questions about his management. Henry wrote to Alexander in New York that Smith senior was spying on him. The younger Smith dismissed his fears as paranoid. 'My dear Henry, As regards that part of your letter in which you say that my father intends setting a watch on your actions, I am sure that either you must have misunderstood your brother or he must have evolved that idea "out of his inner consciousness" as the German did his picture of a camel. From what I know of my father (and you will allow I have had some experience) he is always straightforward and such a vile idea would never enter his head.'

In February 1874, William IV travelled up from his home in Melton Mowbray to talk to Alexander Bruce. 'He was very urgent about limiting the business until the bank account was reduced and the old partners paid out,' Bruce reported to Henry. 'I told him how exceedingly anxious you were and how constantly you were impressing the same thing and the necessity for economy.' But he took the opportunity to express an opinion of his own. 'With this constant pressure from Mr Wm and Mr Smith to restrict the business, would you not still further limit the quantity to be brewed for export, the more so as this is such a very dear year for brewing?'

Henry ignored all the advice he was given, gambling on Black's assurance that he had solved the problems in the Edinburgh breweries. He lost. The October ales refused to clear and Black's only suggestion, to give the beer more time to settle, was little help to a business in deep financial trouble.

On 15 February 1875, David Younger and Alexander Smith told Henry that Bruce should be made a partner. 'You must know that after what Willie

Facing page: criticism of the quality of its beer was reflected in this 1871 letter to Younger's wholesale customers.

CHIEF OFFICES.

EDINBURGH...Abbey Brewery.	CORK.............20, Merchants' Quay.	DERBY.....Cox, Clark & Co., Corn Market.
GLASGOW......14, Queen Street.	NEWCASTLE...97, Pilgrim Street.	DARLINGTON...T. Plews & Son.
ABERDEEN....1, Harriet Street.	LIVERPOOL....1, Seel Street.	LONGTOWN......Brewery Co., nr. Carlisle.
DUBLIN.........16, Bachelor's Walk.	SWANSEA......Quay Parade.	ULVERSTONE...J. Addison, Union Vaults.
BELFAST......5, Gloucester Street.	MANCHESTER.33a, Blackfriars Street.	LONDON........Belvedere Road, Lambeth.

ABBEY AND HOLYROOD BREWERIES,
EDINBURGH, October, 1871.

SIR,

We have again the honour of addressing you at the commencement of another Brewing Season. On this occasion we regret to have to report that the Hop Crop has been a failure as regards quantity, but we are glad to state that the quality is superior.

The Barley Crops are unusually good both in quality and quantity, and excellent for malting. The deficiency in Wheat has, however, had an unfavourable influence on the market price.

Notwithstanding these drawbacks, we are in an unusually good position to supply our friends with the new Season's Brewings of INDIA PALE, MILD, and STRONG ALES, prices of which remain unaltered. Orders for registration we shall feel obliged by receiving as early as possible to prevent disappointment.

We take this opportunity of congratulating the Trade upon their successful opposition to the crude and unjust Licensing Bill introduced last Session, and earnestly trust that the united efforts which they have made will enable them to obtain a satisfactory adjustment of this—to them—vital question, and secure them from further unjustifiable attack, and their property from depreciation.

Thanking you for past favours,

We remain, Sir, Your obedient Servants,

WM. YOUNGER & CO.

PRICES TO THE TRADE.

OCTOBER 1871 TO OCTOBER 1872.

MARKS.	QUALITY.			HHD.	BRL.	KIL.
XP.	INDIA PALE ALE		...	81/-	54/-	27/-
X.	MILD EDINBURGH ALE		...	63/-	42/-	21/-
XX.	DITTO	,,	...	72/-	48/-	24/-
XXX.	DITTO	,,	,,	81/-	54/-	27/-
S.	STRONG	,,	,,	90/-	60/-	30/-
XXXX.	STOCK	,,	,,	99/-	66/-	33/-

BOTTLING ALES.

				HHD.	BRL.	KIL.
XP.	INDIA PALE ALE	...	...	81/-	54/-	27/-
No. 3.	EDINBURGH ALE	...	...	90/-	60/-	30/-
No. 2.	DITTO	...	...	108/-	72/-	36/-
No. 1.	DITTO	...	...	126/-	84/-	42/-
	DINNER ALE	...	...	54/-	—	18/-

Terms—Discount Ten per Cent. for Cash in a Month, Carriage Paid.

South Wales and West of England Stores and Offices, Quay Parade, Swansea.

has now done and what he and Mr Smith have already done for us in the way of security, that we are greatly indebted to them and that they have a right to dictate terms to us. The proposition comes in the first place from Mr Smith and Willie is quite of the same opinion with him. It is that we should assume Bruce as a partner. I am sorry to say that we have greatly lost the confidence of Mr Smith and Willie, so much so that should it not be regained we are utterly and completely at their mercy and were they at any moment to withdraw their security from us, it would be the destruction of our business.'

An illustration from the *Licensed Victuallers' Guardian* in 1872.

Five days later William put the boot in. 'My dear Henry, Davie has I suppose written to tell you of the understanding that Smith and I have come to and I may as well write also, as it remains to be decided whether the business sinks or swims.

'You ask in what way have Smith and I lost confidence in you. I tell you why. You have the lion's share in the business. You are the senior partner and started in the new firm with years of experience which Davie and Aleck Smith had not, so naturally on you must fall the responsibility of the position into which you have allowed the business to fall.

'On examining the accounts, I find that up to 31 Dec 1874 since I left the business, you have spent no less than £14,290 in hard cash, not counting what you have paid in interest, and that in 1871 you spent £3,090 and in 1872 no less than £3,374. You went on expending thousands in advertising, which was just so much money

At the Abbey Brewery, 1876.
Left to right: Alex Smith, Henry Younger, Charles Younger and Alexander Bruce. A year earlier, Bruce had been made a partner and given total control of the brewery. Henry had been sidelined, as a result of his mismanagement. Bruce's apparent detachment from the rest of the group seems to reflect continuing board tension.

thrown away as you were not in a position from want of capital to extend the business. Then you brought in all sorts of expensive reforms as you called them, an expensive brewer in Black, at the same time the working expense at the brewery went on increasing. And lastly, you went on living at a rate quite out of proportion to what you were entitled.

'How do you call that honest? I can tell you that Mr Smith and I do not. Smith says that when the new firm began, he told you that all the partners should put their salaries on a small scale and you talked of £1,000 for yourself and £500 for the others. Were the capital your own, I would have no right to interfere with your expenditure. But surely, when you owe some £15,000, I have a right to say that you must keep down your expenditure to a reasonable sum and repay me the money which I never meant to be with you for an indefinite period. Knowing the crippled state of the business, I thought you next door to a madman to pay £50 for a gun, for which you had no earthly use. And Davie tells me you paid £50 for a diamond to indulge your fancy when you were on the verge of bankruptcy.

'When we gave in 1870 the Bill to the City for £40,000, you all faithfully promised to do everything in your powers to reduce the balance at the Bank, and what do we find by the Books? You have actually spent £5,000

Below: during the 19th century the pub evolved from a single room without a bar, to become a place not only to drink, but to dine and entertain. In this *Punch* cartoon, the waiter remonstrates with the customers who are involved in a heated discussion, 'Gentlemen, gentlemen! – order I beg – recollect you're in a public house!'

on extra casks, increasing the overdraft to £51,000. I plainly tell you that owing to the current reports, the directors of the Bank took fright and unless I had agreed to become security for another £20,000, Smith assures me that the business could not have gone on.

'Smith wanted me to telegraph for you. I dread to think of the scene had you met him in this temper and I got it put off. But he and I made up our minds of the steps for our own defence and Bruce taken in as a partner was the result. The proposal that Mr Smith makes is that you should relinquish a share of the profit in favour of Bruce . . . If Bruce gets two sixteenths, it will be equal to £15,000 of capital. So I propose HY: 6/16, DY 4/16, AS 4/16. Bruce 2/16 = 16/16.

'There is only one alternative for you. Agree to Smith's and my proposal or bring the business to a standstill.'

Henry was in a state of panic. As well as his own and the company's financial problems, his wife had died the previous year, leaving him with five motherless children (he swiftly remarried and fathered four more). He still would not accept that Younger's plight was his fault. He was not responsible for the beer going bad. Making Bruce a partner would not make any difference to that problem, which was more in the nature of an act of God. But he was in no position to resist. Alexander Bruce's partnership was formally announced on 21 May 1875, backdated to 1 January to give him a full share in the year's profits.

By then he was already living in Edinburgh and had effectively become Younger's chief executive. Aged 35, Bruce took total control of the brewery and its trade, beginning by reading all the mail each morning and presiding with calm authority over every aspect of the business.

His first task was to weather the immediate financial crisis. William IV and Andrew Smith's additional guarantees had extended Younger's overdraft to £60,000, but the bank made it clear that this was the limit. At the beginning of May, it looked as though the company was not going to be able to keep within it. Henry, who had moved to London, was terrified. Bruce tried to assuage his fears. 'Dear Sir,' he wrote on 4 May, 'Bank. Do not be anxious too much regarding Thursday. If the N'castle & Baird's bills are accepted in time, the Sixty will be reached. Mr Bain of the Bank gave me one grain of comfort upon leaving him on 30th April – not to be too anxious, so this shows we have his right side. I am certainly very desirous that he should see his confidence is not misplaced. He said he was very glad I was in Edinburgh, not meaning, I am sure, to throw the slightest reflection on Mr Cuthbert.'

'Pale ale. The harshness or bitterness of some brewings this season arises, I think, chiefly from the very high price of hops, necessitating the use of an inferior class. Now that the price has fallen, the better qualities are used much more freely and will be so all through the summer.

'I know it is and will for a long time be a most anxious time for us, but I have confidence that if we can only pull respectably through this season, everything will be right. Mr Alex. Smith is more hopeful and I think we should accept as a good sign the evident interest his father now takes. It will give all others confidence. I do hope you will not get too nervous. The cooler and quieter we all keep the better.'

Bruce himself kept admirably cool under the financial fire, with the result that at the end of of June 1875, Younger's had made a trading profit of £9,484 for the year. It was a poor result, but it was much better than the

At the Abbey and Holyrood Brewery, early 1870s. The company fire brigade and, *facing page*, Holyrood brewery workers.

Detail of 'Mixing malt', from Gustave Doré's *London*, c.1870.

Left: a London brewery c.1875 and, *right*, mash tuns and coppers in a French brewery of the same period.

£628 made in 1873/4 or the £7,145 earned in 1872/3, which would have been a loss of more than £3,500 but for the transfer of a surplus of £11,600 held in London.

The latest results had also been achieved in spite of extremely high prices for hops. Alex Cuthbert was filled with admiration for Bruce's management and considered the corner had been turned. But the new managing partner was less optimistic. Younger's production overheads were far too heavy in relationship to its diminished output, but with export markets down and turnover in the south-east of England static, there was little point to any sales drive. And in the north-west, the recent large investment in Liverpool had yet to begin earning its keep. The company's acute shortage of capital also meant that Mitchell had had to be told to defer any promotion that cost money.

On the surface, Bruce remained as mild-mannered as ever. But there were signs of his new status. For example, he began to address Henry with a fraction more familiarity as 'Mr Younger'. And, more dramatically, he married Agnes Livingstone, the daughter of Dr David Livingstone, the famous missionary to Africa. Within months of arriving in Edinburgh, Alexander Bruce had not only rescued Younger's from collapse, he had become a personage in polite society.

He still had a great deal to put right, however, before the company could be said to be out of danger. Apart from staying solvent, the most important step was to cure the persistent sourness afflicting so much of Younger's beers.

Scottish brewers had shared in the progress made in brewing technology in the second half of the 19th century, but up to 1870 most advances had been in mechanical processes for mashing, boiling and refrigerating the liquor. Most breweries used steam power and temperatures were monitored

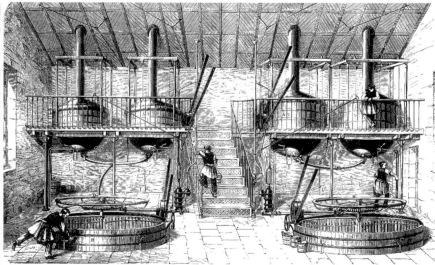

by thermometers, with saccharometers measuring the sugar content and gravity of the beer. And ice machines employing a variety of coolants, such as ether, carbon dioxide or hydrocarbons, were beginning to be installed.

Understanding of the chemistry of brewing, though, was still limited. Although Louis Pasteur had been making discoveries in biochemistry for nearly 20 years, it was only in 1876 that he published a synthesis of his work on yeast cultures, fermentation and what was to become known as pasteurisation. *Etudes sur la Bière* revolutionised the manufacture of beer and within a short time most breweries employed a chemist. Younger's hired its first, a young man named William McCowan, in November 1877, and the following summer sent him off with Andrew Thomson to spy out the latest developments in Europe.

They began by visiting Ulm College to see Pasteur, but discovered the famous scientist was in Italy. However, his assistant showed them Pasteur's laboratory and the prototype plant for his new system of brewing. McCowan reported that this essentially consisted of a closed fermenting vat and cleansing vessel from which the finished beer was drawn. 'On enquiry as to its applicability on the large scale, our answer was the usual Continental shrug of the shoulders.'

Louis Pasteur's discoveries in biochemistry revolutionised the brewing process.

They next called on the Pneumatic Malting Co. in Paris, only to find that the people they needed to see there were in London. 'However, we were permitted to see a process which as far as we could gather was Galland's (malting) system with improvements by Mr Gruber, brewer of Strasbourg. But we did not obtain any data which could be considered reliable enough to enable you to form an opinion on the process.' Oddly, McCowan found Younger's ale in Paris much healthier than in its London stores. His experiments when he returned to Scotland also revealed that the company's yeasts were better than those in most other breweries in Edinburgh, although still not as pure as he thought they should be. Obviously, only a new brewing system would enable Younger's to get rid of the bitterness that its beer was still justly complained of. 'Experiments are being carried out to overcome this evil without at the same time sacrificing our present good qualities.' McCowan concluded, 'PS. We purpose treating some barrels of beer by Pasteur's method tomorrow or Wednesday.'

Younger's main concern, however, remained its finances. At the end of 1878, the situation was as crucial as ever, largely because Scotland's banks

The failure of the City of Glasgow Bank, October 1878 – 'the greatest disaster that had ever befallen the commercial community of Great Britain.'

were themselves in trouble. Wearily, Bruce wrote to Henry: 'If anxiety to have it paid off would have cancelled the debt, long since this it would have been wiped out. After the experience of the British Linen, I think we have all felt it precarious trusting too much in any bank and this stoppage of the City of Glasgow and the tightness all the Scotch banks have since exhibited shows there has been too good grounds for our fears. The loan to Chas. Bell & the Abbey property purchase, both at the time considered by all judicious if not a necessity, have certainly postponed payments to Mr William. Could any of us have anticipated such a crisis, neither of these transactions would have been entered into. Now that we are in the very heart of the crisis, the end of which none can foretell, it occasions us great anxiety as our collections are very bad and all our customers are complaining of the want of money.

'Last year from 1 January to May, the Bank account ran up £24,000 or so, but our requirements this season will be the same or thereabouts, with the unfortunate prospect of money much worse to get in. Fortunately, we have the letter from the Bank of Scotland agreeing to an overdraft of from £20,000 to £25,000 with security during your buying season, but the way they criticise every Bill for discount lets us see how watchful and circumspect we must be. The next six months will be a time of great anxiety, as it will be one continual run of barley payments and malt duties, with comparatively little coming in. But after that solid payments should be made.'

The letter concluded: 'Regarding Mr Smith's position with the City of Glasgow Bank, the final call of £250 must be paid on Saturday.'

The failure of the City of Glasgow Bank on 2 October 1878 was described by one contemporary commentator as 'the greatest disaster that had ever befallen the commercial community of Great Britain'. This was an exaggeration, but not an absurd one. Founded in 1839 as a mutual society, the bank catered especially for small investors, with its branches opening in the evenings to take deposits. At the annual general meeting in June 1878, the directors reported that deposits were up to £8M and that a dividend of 12 per cent was to be paid, approximately four times the return on government gilt-edged stocks. Rumours that the bank was seeking help from its competitors began to spread in August, but no one anticipated its sudden collapse. Only later did it emerge that the accountant appointed by the other Scottish banks to investigate the City of Glasgow's affairs had found them in such a bad state that he had advised against any attempt at a rescue.

The impact on the bank's 1,200 shareholders was calamitous, as their liability was unlimited. When they met in Glasgow City Hall to accept the bank's voluntary liquidation with debts of over £6m., they knew that almost without exception they were ruined. Among their number was Andrew Smith's younger son, Andrew II, who had inherited his recently deceased father's holding in the bank as part of his legacy. Smith senior's stake in Younger's had gone to Alexander, which should have meant that the brewing company was unaffected. Quixotically, though, Alexander had underwritten his brother's debts. The bank's receiver had already made two calls of £250 on Andrew II, but there was no knowing what his final liability would total. It might even bankrupt the brewery.

In January 1879, the directors of the bank went on trial in Edinburgh's High Court. They included a former deputy-lieutenant of Morayshire, a Glasgow bailie, a shipowner and a distiller. Some were prominent members of the Church of Scotland. Although the Lord Justice-Clerk decided that their mismanagement of the bank's funds was probably not for personal advantage, the prosecution revealed that large, unsecured loans had been made to insolvent companies with which some of its board were associated. All the directors were found guilty and sentenced to prison for terms from eight to 18 months.

'All our business engagements have to be entered into with Mr Smith's position kept in mind,' Bruce warned Henry and David. 'It hampers us on every side. Mr Smith's capital at his credit is £62,000. In the event of death, bankruptcy or insolvency, this has to be paid out in ten half-yearly instalments, which would be say £12,000 per annum.'

Unlike most of Scotland's financial community, Bruce refused to panic. He already knew that a relief committee of the 'principal men' of Glasgow, Edinburgh and Aberdeen had promised to help the liquidator recover as much as possible; they did their work so well that within two years the bank's creditors had been paid 18s. in the £.

This happy outcome, though, was a long way off for Andrew II, who for a time lived on a small allowance from his brother. It was equally distant for Younger's, still desperately short of capital of its own and struggling to cope with a downturn in demand for beer. Regardless, Bruce pursued his twin targets of economy and reliability with grim determination. Gradually, the financial pressure eased and the efforts to improve Younger's manufacturing standards gained ground. On 19 January 1880, Henry sent Bruce a brief note. It read: 'All the ales received (in London) simply <u>lovely</u>.' And ten days later he congratulated Bruce on the results for the previous six months.

Bruce was delighted. For nearly five years he had put up with an endless stream of complaints from Henry about Younger's beer and Younger's finances. 'I cannot express to you the satisfaction it has given me to receive your note of approbation over the balance,' he wrote back. 'There is also a great sense of relief about the future, which I know from the general tone of our correspondence you share, as I am sure we both feel that, although public houses are being bought up right and left, we are more completely masters of our business than any of our neighbours.'

'Come Fill Me a Tankard': George Leybourne, the original 'Champagne Charlie', was a celebrated comic singer, at the forefront of music hall entertainment which was burgeoning in Victorian England. The subject of this song sheet – dedicated to Younger's – is appropriate, since music halls originated in pubs.

BREWING TODAY

The Tadcaster Brewery brews John Smith's, the United Kingdom's best-selling ale, and other Scottish Courage beers. Founded in 1883, the building houses state-of-the-art plant, including a high-speed canning line and recently much-expanded production capacity.

6

Never More
Encouraging

In 1886 Arthur Guinness & Son went public for £6m. The share issue was
oversubscribed 28 times and the starting gun had been fired for the great
Victorian brewing boom. Henry Younger and Alexander Bruce both
participated in the issue, more than doubling their money when they sold
their Guinness holdings a year later for 276s. a share.

The attractions of taking their own companies to the stock market were
instantly obvious to the directors of every brewery in the United Kingdom.
At a stroke, they could raise extra capital to expand their operations and
substantially increase the market value of their own holdings. Younger's
was the first Scottish brewery to follow Guinness's example, becoming a
limited liability company on 17 August 1887, with an authorised capital of
£1M, of which half was in £100 ordinary shares and half in new £100
preference shares.

As usual, Alexander Bruce was the driving force, selecting the London
stockbroking firm of Seymour Pierce Chalk as the issuing house and
providing all the necessary information for the prospectus. This began with
an unequivocal claim that 'the business was first established at the Abbey
Brewery, Edinburgh, in the year 1749 by an ancestor of Mr Henry Johnston
Younger, the Chairman of the present Company, and has ever since that
date been continued in the same premises.' More accurate, as well as more
relevant, was the record of recent progress, which showed that Younger's
production had risen from 90,000 barrels in 1881 to 215,000 barrels in 1886,
approximately one-sixth of all Scottish beer brewed that year. Production of
Guinness, for the record, was 1.4M barrels, more than all Scotland's output.

Following Pasteur's biochemical discoveries, brewing became increasingly scientific. *Above*: Younger's laboratory, photographed in 1890, and a microscope slide from the same lab.

Holyrood Brewery, from *Barnard's Noted Breweries of Great Britain and Ireland* published in 1889.

Such a large increase in production inevitably involved heavy expenditure on new plant and equipment. Both the Holyrood and the Abbey Breweries needed further expansion and development, while Younger's maltings had spread into half a dozen buildings, including some as far away as Moray Park. The company's production of bottled beer had also grown enormously, with a large part of Younger's storerooms next to the Queen's Park taken up by its bottling floor, described by Alfred Barnard, the author of *Barnard's Noted Breweries*, as: 'a very animated scene, thronged with busy workers. At one end scores of crates of new bottles were being unpacked and their contents taken to the washing division . . . before being filled. The washing apparatus consists of a circular iron frame revolving on its own axis, whereon are placed twelve bottles upside down over a nozzle, through which rises a powerful stream of water which, after a few revolutions, cleans the bottles perfectly. They are then placed neck downwards in a tray on wheels and taken to the filling division, where the beer is bottled. In this place a number of men are seated in front of a board, like the keyboard of a piano, through which project taps connected with hose, lain on direct to the store-casks in the next apartment. Before reaching the apparatus, where eight bottles are filled at one time, the beer passes through several muslin strainers to collect every little atom of sediment (should there be any), as the beer must be absolutely brilliant . . . Proceeding a few yards to the left, we come to a place where the bottles are corked by a method similar to that adopted by the great claret houses of Bordeaux, each machine corking 100 dozen per hour. In the next division the bottles are wired, then capsuled and labelled "The Monk Brand".'

It was Bruce, too, who sorted out the inevitable 'blow up' from Henry Younger, this time about George Stenhouse, the head brewer, becoming a director. 'Did GS ever express a wish to share in the risks of the business when not as flourishing as at present?' Henry argued hotly. But his real objection was the fact that 'from time to time he acted most rudely to me, especially when merchants and strangers have been present, never at times even acknowledging my presence.' The chairman had nothing against Bruce's suggestion that James Belfrage, the firm's London manager, also joined the board. And of course he had no complaint about his own son, Harry, becoming a director at the age of 18. Bruce's younger brother Robert, incidentally, was appointed secretary of the newly incorporated company. At the first general meeting on 21 September, the chairman revealed that 3,363 preference shares had been allotted privately, increasing the number of shareholders to 73. All the ordinary share capital issued, however, was retained by the original partners, except for a small percentage allocated to the new directors. And even this had to be sold back on their deaths.

Next but one to incorporate under the 1882/6 Companies Act was McEwan's, on 24 July 1889, also for £1m., the only other Scottish brewer to reach this magic figure. In McEwan's case, the founder retained 43,000 of the 50,000 £10 ordinary shares. His sister's fourth son William Younger, who had become McEwan's managing director, was allotted 5,000 and her third, a lawyer named Robert, was given 1,000. The remaining 1,000 was shared equally between James Molleson, McEwan's accountant, and William Hunter, the new company's secretary. All the 50,000 new £10 preference shares were offered for sale to the public through the British Linen Bank. McEwan's prospectus showed: 'Assets: Casks £38,000. Bottles £5,600. Barley £5,000. Malt £19,000. Hops £13,000. Total £91,000. Ale: Home £24,000. Export £78,000. Money owed by customers £199,000, of which home: £68,000. Overseas £131,000. Cash £6,000. The whole of the property and plant appearing as balances in Mr McEwan's books, as well as that portion of the price representing the cost to the company of the goodwill of the business and trade marks £591,000. Total £1m.'

McEwan's first general meeting was on 15 November 1889, by which time £300,000 had been paid up by new preference shareholders. A final instalment of £4 per share, to make up the balance of £200,000 still owing, was due on 2 December, but with the new preference shares quoted at a premium on the London and Edinburgh Stock Exchanges, there was no doubt about its receipt, especially as William McEwan announced that 'Since the formation of the company four months ago, the business has steadily increased, the sales being greater than during the corresponding month in any year since the origin of the concern, and that as far as I can judge the prospects were never more encouraging than at the present time.' The new shareholders applauded loudly and their 63-year-old millionaire chairman could not help smiling through his patriarchal beard; he did have a child, a stepdaughter named Margaret, by then a young woman. McEwan had married her mother Helen Anderson in 1885.

By the end of 1889, most of the bigger breweries had become limited liability companies with publicly quoted shares, including all the English giants such as Bass, Courage, Watney and Whitbread. All that was left was a scattering of small fry not large enough to float on their own, like John Barras and Reid Brothers in Newcastle.

The Barras brewery had done well enough over the past 40 years, during most of which it had been managed by John jnr's nephew, Charles Reed, who

Brand protection was becoming increasingly important. A letter from Younger's to 'merchants and importers' requesting them to check names and labels.

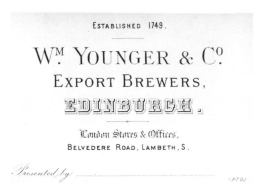

ESTABLISHED 1749.

W.^{M.} YOUNGER & C.^{O.}
EXPORT BREWERS,
EDINBURGH.

London Stores & Offices,
BELVEDERE ROAD, LAMBETH, S.

Presented by
(P.T.O)

Younger's trade calling card, early 1890s.

The earliest form of motorised road transport. The John Smith Tadcaster Brewery, as part of the Courage group, joined Scottish & Newcastle plc in 1995.

had been in sole charge since John Barras jnr died in 1861. Ownership of the brewery, however, had been left in trust during the life of John III, who lived for another 21 years. On his death, Charles Reed bought Barras's 18 public houses, but it was another six years before the Gateshead brewery was sold for a modest £8,500 to the North Eastern Railway. Reed himself had not been interested. He had already purchased a much larger brewery in Bath Lane, Newcastle. The Tyne Brewery had been built regardless of expense in 1868 and by 1882 was producing more beer than any other in the North-East. Too much, indeed, for the local market, and it had gone bankrupt. Charles Reed bought it from the receiver. In 1884, following an extensive modernisation programme, the 1770 foundation stone from Barras's old brewery at Gateshead was ferried across the river and built into a new brewer's house at the Tyne Brewery as the finishing touch.

By then, Reed was a provincial grandee, deputy lieutenant of County Durham, an honorary colonel in the Northumberland militia and about to become a Companion of the Bath. The hard work was done by Thomas Lovibond, a third-generation London brewer who, almost uniquely for the time, was also a Fellow of the Institute of Chemistry. Reed poached him from Richardson's Brewery in Newark in 1887 and within two years Lovibond had transformed the quality and reputation of Barras's beer.

John Barras & Co. was incorporated with an authorised capital of £180,000 in March 1889. Charles Reed, who held over 93 per cent of the original capital, was keen to realise his investment. During 1889, he sold over half his £10 ordinary shares to various individuals, including 401 to his second son, Barras Reed, who had been appointed the company secretary on a salary of £200 a year, and 500 to Lovibond. But that still left Charles Reed with over 40 per cent of Barras & Co.'s equity. Discreet enquiries flushed out several potential buyers, including Younger's.

Alexander Bruce was already talking to William Reid about turning Reid Brothers into a limited liability company, with himself and Harry Younger on the board and the Newcastle firm's long-standing credit for purchases of Scotch ale from the Edinburgh brewery converted into shares. A letter from William Reid in June 1888, however, revealed that he was negotiating with John Barras and with James and William Allison, who between them owned two breweries, one in North Shields and the other at Monkwearmouth in Sunderland, as well as a string of pubs and off-licences, about a possible merger, and that an outright purchase of either was only a matter of price. Bruce made a direct approach to Charles Reed and found out that he valued his business at £168,000. Bruce thought this far too much, although he did not break off communications. But in truth the last thing he wanted was a major production unit on the Tyne. The great attraction of Newcastle to all the leading Scottish breweries, as to those in Burton-on-Trent, was that it was such a good market for their own beers. Reid Brothers, indeed, had become little more than Younger's local agent.

A deal with the Allisons came much closer to fruition. By the end of December 1888, Younger's had upped its opening offer of £90,000 to £117,000 and the following July Bruce was all set to visit Newcastle to finalise terms. But three months later the deal was still hanging fire, with the brothers insisting on excluding the Clarendon Hotel in North Shields. As this was only valued at £800, it seemed a trifling reason for Younger's to pull out. But it coincided with Bruce's receipt of an independent valuation of Barras's Tyne Brewery. The canny Scot had been hoping to pull off the double merger all along, but only if it was cheap enough.

The breakdown did not stop Younger's going ahead with plans to issue two-thirds of its own preference shares to the public at a price of £105 a share, to raise around £350,000. When the offer closed on 30 July 1890, it was subscribed three times over.

In the meantime, Barras and the Allison brothers had been approached by a deal-maker named Hugh Cumberland, a London partner of the Canadian financier H. O'Hagan. Cumberland suggested that if the Allisons and Barras merged with other local brewers and licensed victuallers, he could float them all together as a public company. On 1 April 1890, J. J. and W. H. Allison, John Barras, Carr Bros & Carr, another North Shields partnership, and wine and spirits merchants Swinburne & Co., combined as Newcastle Breweries, with an authorised capital of £200,000 ordinary shares, £200,000 preference and £300,000 in debentures. All three categories were oversubscribed and Cumberland introduced them at a small premium on the London and Newcastle Stock Exchanges.

Among the new group's assets was a contract giving it a 42.5 per cent discount on purchases of McEwan's ale, with a further 2.5 per cent if the trade exceeded £14,000 a year. No wonder Alexander Bruce discouraged Reid Brothers from becoming part of Newcastle Breweries by offering the firm an exclusive 15-year agency for Younger's beers from the date it became a limited company. This finally took place in September 1891, with Younger's taking up £40,000 in shares and debentures.

That did not make Newcastle Breweries any less potent a threat. The new group had two big advantages. One was the combination of Thomas Lovibond, who became the group's first managing director, and Barras's recently modernised Tyne Brewery, which the prospectus made clear would, in time, produce all the beer required by the new combine's customers. For the first time in Newcastle's history, local beers were beginning to rival imports in quality as well as quantity.

The other was the 215 licensed properties that the five firms (the Allisons had two companies) brought into their merger. The main reason why many brewers had rushed to go public was to raise money to finance expanding their tied markets. The result of this competition was a dramatic rise in the value of public house leases, in many cases well above their real value. By and large Scottish brewers, thanks to the historic aversion of local magistrates to tied houses, were spared this temptation. Although not entirely.

Col. Sir Charles Reed, chairman and major shareholder of John Barras & Co.

Appointed by Charles Reed in 1887, Thomas Lovibond transformed the quality of Barras's beer.

BREWING TODAY

Tyne Brewery, *right, top and bottom*: the new bottling line, installed in 1996, produces 24,000 bottles of Newcastle Brown every hour, 24 hours a day, five days a week. *Top left*: vehicles awaiting loading;

middle left: the present brewhouse, opened in 1994. *Bottom left*: in addition to sophisticated computerised monitoring, regular sample tasting and viewing is still an essential part of quality control.

The Tyne Brewery, built in 1868.

Younger's, for example, bought eight pubs in and around Bishopswearmouth from William Allison in 1887 and continued to acquire leases in the North-East during the 1890s. But many English brewers were to rue the high prices they paid to extend their ties with public houses. Newcastle Breweries, in contrast, acquired its pubs at a historic valuation.

Not that this situation lasted. The ink had scarcely dried on Newcastle Breweries's new share certificates before Hugh Cumberland put into action phase two of O'Hagan's plan for the group. Northern Breweries Corporation was formed in November 1891, as a vehicle for the public houses belonging to Newcastle Breweries. At the end of its first year, Northern Breweries Corporation had spent £53,000 on buying pub leases and by the beginning of 1899 its portfolio was valued at nearly £250,000. That year it doubled to £510,000, following the acquisition by Newcastle Breweries of two more local breweries, W. A. Falconar & Co. of Howdon-on-Tyne and John Sanderson & Sons of the Haymarket. Both had their own tied houses, which were transferred into Northern Breweries Corporation. So were the off-licences belonging to a Newcastle wine and spirit merchant, James Routledge, bought at the same time. By 1900, Northern Breweries Corporation controlled more than 300 licensed premises, financed by £200,000 in preference shares, £100,000 in mortgage debentures and a £150,000 bank loan. (In January 1903, the company dropped the word Breweries from its name to become the Northern Corporation.)

Prospectuses for Newcastle Breweries, John Barras & Co., and Northern Breweries, plus the first annual report of The Newcastle Breweries Limited.

Younger's advertisement, *above*, in a Berlin exhibition. *Below*: the label on which the sign is based.

By then, Lovibond had centralised most of Newcastle Breweries' beer production at the Tyne Brewery, where a new extension had increased capacity by 50 per cent, merged the Swinburne, Routledge and Falconar wines and spirits businesses, and built a new plant to make aerated mineral water, another Falconar interest. With the UK economy once more enjoying the doubtful benefits of an economic boom, after more than twenty years of falling prices (in 1896, most retail prices reached their lowest levels for 200 years), the brewing industry on both sides of the border could be forgiven for anticipating ever greater prosperity.

Admittedly, there were a few clouds on the horizon. One of the darkest was the unremitting pressure from the temperance movement. *The Temperance Witness*, for example, had published a black list of all Newcastle Breweries' shareholders, and the city's drinks industry had been reviled as causing 'the greatest hindrance to the spread of everything good and the great increase of everything that is evil.' And prohibition was becoming a major political issue, with an unending flow of 'permissive' bills brought before Parliament.

The biggest shock had come in 1891, when the House of Lords had rejected an appeal by Mrs Sharpe, the owner of a public house in a remote part of Westmorland, against her local magistrates for refusing to renew her licence. The right of JPs to cancel licences was finally enshrined in law and Alexander Bruce warned Younger's regional representatives of 'the extreme action of Licensing Magistrates following thereon, which render it necessary that applications for loans be put forward only in very urgent cases and where the risks are reduced to a minimum.'

But the industry was fighting back. Harry Younger spent most of his time promoting the interests of the licensed trade. He was a member of the Parliamentary Committee of the Scottish Licensed Trade Defence Association and of the industry's Joint Wholesale and Retail Parliamentary Committee in London. He chaired innumerable fund-raising trade banquets around the country. And in 1895, he stood for Parliament in East Edinburgh, halving the sitting member's majority.

William McEwan was even more influential. He had held Central Edinburgh for William Gladstone's Liberal Party since 1886 and his pragmatic opinions carried considerable weight behind the scenes, although he was no orator and never spoke in the House of Commons.

The brewers also won themselves support by their generosity. McEwan's gift of an academical hall to Edinburgh University, announced in 1887 and opened 10 years later, cost him £115,000 (say £7.5m. today). More modestly, Younger's donated £1,000 towards a professorship in public health at Edinburgh University. Another £500 was contributed for the celebration of Queen Victoria's Diamond Jubilee the same year. Every brewer in the country gave generously to this historic event, secure in the knowledge that the nation's celebrations would involve many glasses being raised to Her Majesty.

As well as influencing public opinion by a general policy of political influence and openhandedness, the drinks industry was also ready to take direct action against its opponents, whatever the cost. When the Head Constable of Tynemouth opposed an appeal by eight publicans against the loss of their licences, Newcastle Breweries financed a successful action against the Town Council for paying his expenses (£132 5s.) on the grounds that the Licensing Act did not allow the council to spend a penny of ratepayers' money in opposing the renewal of licences, and that the Watch Committee had nothing to do with carrying out the licensing laws in the borough.

Tynemouth appealed to the Court of Appeal and lost again, at which point it decided to give up. Its defeat, however, meant that however badly a public house was run, no municipal authority anywhere in the UK could pay for the local police to oppose the renewal of its licence. The City of Liverpool was so concerned that it offered to support an appeal by Tynemouth to the House of Lords. Their Lordships' judgment was finally delivered on 16 May 1899. It began promisingly for the municipalities, with Lord MacNaughton declaring it might not unduly strain the language of the licensing acts to accept: 'That the proper regulation of licensed houses within a borough is essential to its good government and to the peace and quiet of the inhabitants.' But he was forced to conclude that the administration of the licensing laws lay with local magistrates, and municipal councils had no right to take on themselves any of the functions of justices of the peace. Newcastle Breweries had won a famous victory.

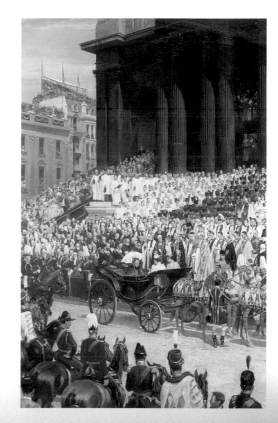

Queen Victoria's Diamond Jubilee celebration at St Paul's Cathedral, 1897.

McEwan Hall, built for Edinburgh University as a gift from William McEwan, and opened in 1897.

7

To Make a Saint Swear

The dawn of the 20th century was a cloudier period than The Empire On Which The Sun Never Set anticipated. What began as just another colonial police action, this time in the Transvaal and the Orange Free State of South Africa, turned into a protracted and bloody conflict taking a frightful toll of British lives. One of them was David Younger's son, another David, a captain in the Gordon Highlanders. A posthumous VC did little to soften his family's grief.

The war also ended the economic boom and English brewers soon found their recently extended ties with public houses a liability, with many tenants unable even to pay interest on the loans they had been given. More and more went bankrupt, forcing the brewers to take possession of their pubs.

Scottish brewers were less affected, but even they were hit by bad debts and falling demand. Younger's was one of the worst troubled, owing to a misguided decision in 1903 to open a bottling plant in London. This was a complete disaster which lasted less than a year and left the company with 48,000 unused bottles. Harry's younger brother Archie was sent south to sort out the mess and collect money owed to Younger's by London publicans. James Belfrage was deeply mortified and retired a couple of years later.

His departure left the day-to-day management of the company in the hands of George Stenhouse and Robert Bruce, as Alexander Bruce had died of pneumonia following on from 'flu in 1893, at the relatively young age of 54. They were both conscientious and hard-working, but they lacked Alexander's flair.

The Café Royal, Edinburgh, opened in 1826, undergoing a series of alterations which left it with some classic *fin de siècle* interior decoration, including tiled murals and stained-glass windows depicting celebrated people (*left*). It exemplifies the way in which pubs were becoming increasingly genteel meeting places.

2nd May 1907

My dear Uncle,

I have your letter of 29th ult which I have read with much interest. It is, as you say, a scandalous shame that that man's licence in Dundee should have been taken away on a first conviction, and instead of being fined £5000, as you vividly put it, for a first offence, he has really been fined £7,500, for, in addition to the £5000 of a bond, he had £2500 of his own in the business. It is to be hoped the Appeal Court will rectify such a flagrant set of injustices, but something similar has already been going on in Glasgow. A poor man had his license taken away the other day for no reason whatever against either a himself or the house, but simply because the Justices thought the district was a congested one and the house ought to be shut. The poor man cried out they might as well put their hand in his pocket and rob him, for he had put the savings of 25 years into the business, and this decision left him in the street - a ruined man. This harshness has caused a good deal of remark, and, if you will look in today's "Scotsman", you will see a description of what happened in Glasgow yesterday, where the feeling culminated in something like a riot at the Licensing Court, which got to such a pitch that the proposed Court had to be abandoned. Feeling seemed to have run very high, but if this rioting succeeds in attracting public attention to these scandals, it may have very far-reaching effects.

I enclose the April sales, which show a fair increase, especially in Glasgow, and I hope we shall now move away in the West Country, which has been a dead weight now for some time. The Military trade too is doing well, mainly caused by us having secured, as I have already told you, the Scots Greys at Piershill and the Seaforth Highlanders at the Castle.

The blot on this sheet is the returns. This has been caused by that movement in the beer I have been telling you about, and it really is a black shame how publicans simply throw the beer back on your hands without any reason at all. You will understand for what a trivial cause they return now when over 200 barrels of these returns have already been sent out again either as ordinary beer or racked beer. I have seen any number of samples of them. The great bulk of them come bright in three days and brilliant in six days, and it is enough to make a saint swear that such beer

should come back at all, but the trade has now got into such a state, these publicans think they can do anything they like.

Harvey has not opened with any clubs yet. These private accounts are just private people. Since I wrote about him he has been working the Swansea district, but he finds it very uphill work owing to the generalxtying of houses. He has only sold one barrel and a half, but he has got good promises from several free houses against his next visit, and I hope these promises will be realised.

We are still in bitterly cold weather, and the sales up to now this week are just holding their own.

I expected Edward Strauss here today, but he has not put in an appearance yet.

I am,
Yours affectionately

W. M'Ewan Esq.,
Cannes.

One of William Younger's numerous letters during 1907 to his uncle, William McEwan, keeping him informed of events in the business.

McEwan's, in contrast, was still run by its founder's shrewd and experienced nephew, William Younger, by then in his fifties. William McEwan himself had retired from politics in 1900 at the age of 73, richer than ever. (In 1906, he gave Polesden Lacey, a Regency villa near Dorking in Surrey, now owned by the National Trust, to his daughter Margaret, who had married the Honourable Ronald Greville in 1891. She had it extensively rebuilt in 1906 to accommodate her celebrated house parties, which included the Royal family, and her collection of paintings, porcelain, furniture and silver are still on display there.) But William McEwan's interest in his brewing business was as keen as ever and his nephew kept him abreast of every development, even when he escaped to the South of France, as in the winter of 1907:

'21 Jan: My dear Uncle, I told you some time ago about Messrs Melvin's proposal that we should take over their loans, seeing that they intend to retire from business. They are to stop brewing at the end of February and Melvin is to endeavour to transfer all his tied trade to us at our prices, without us being required to take over any of the loans. If, at the end of four months, he should desire to sell up any, we are to have the option of taking over any we may desire. The whole trade involved is about £8,000 per annum, mostly pale ale.

'You will remember that for many years (Melvin) malted for us at Bonington, while for the last two years we have taken over his maltings entirely at a rent, much to his relief.

'4 Feb: During my 31 years experience in this brewery, we have not had such an attack of acidity since the autumn of 1882, just after the Egyptian trouble, when the beer went sour in the tuns. The six months ending 1905 seem like a nightmare to me even now, for during three months of that time I was totally blind in one eye and the other was so dimmed by overuse that I could hardly discern an object on the other side of the street and it was while I was in that helpless state that the acidity had to be fought. While brewing science has made great strides in the last twenty years, it has not yet reached the pitch where it can be relied upon as a certain guide. The nose and the palate are still required to be the ultimate Court of Appeal.

'27 Feb: Melvin called today with a list of his Glasgow customers, most of whom, he reported, are likely to take our beer, more or less on our own terms. Teacher, his largest customer, who takes from him £4,000 a year, has practically come to terms with us and a trial order goes to him today. He will be quite a fish worth landing.

'Montagu Baird has been here today to repeat what I have already heard since my return, that there is something like consternation not only in the brewing trade but in the allied trades at what is understood to be the intention of the Government in the new Licensing Bill for England. The result is that these allied trades are combining outside the brewing organisations to make independent attacks on the Members of Parliament for their various districts to try to ensure something like fair treatment for the license (*sic*) holder. I am told that up to last week Herbert Gladstone's idea was to impose a time limit of fifteen years upon all existing licences, after which they were all to lapse to the State and any houses that were to be allowed to remain open would have to be redeemed by their present owners at a monopoly price. It seems the Government Broker went to the Home Office and explained to Herbert Gladstone that if that was his intention it would cause an absolute collapse of all brewing securities, and he seems to have succeeded in frightening him, for I hear now the latest scheme is that, while they retain the 15-year limit, all licences after that are to remain at the absolute discretion of the magistrates. The latter, of course, is bad enough, but if the other scheme had been carried out it is questionable if even the Debenture Holders in the various English Breweries could have been paid out.

'4 Mar: I have seen numerous candidates this forenoon for a vacancy we have in the Dundee district for a traveller in room of Mr Robertson, whom we have had to get quit of. He was going wrong and neglecting his duty. I enclose the February sales, which are disappointing. I suppose we must blame the weather, for you will notice by the smallness of returns how steady the beer has been, and 2 per cent of returns in these days when customers all over the country claim the right to return "bottoms", which we do not always succeed in defeating, is really about low water mark.

The Hon. Mrs Ronald Greville, William McEwan's stepdaughter, to whom he gave Polesden Lacey, Surrey, *below*.

Scenes from the Fountain
Brewery in the 1900s. *Above,*
loading barrels onto drays;
below: the cooperage.

PS. I wonder if this great upheaval at the London County Council elections will have the effect of making the Government hesitate before they introduce too drastic proposals in their Licensing Bill?

'8 Mar: I don't know if I told you that the various Brewers Associations in Scotland, the Edinburgh Association, the Glasgow Association and the Country Associations, have all combined and pooled their funds in order to be the better able to counteract the machinations of the extreme temperance reformers. I have just been informed that at a full meeting of the Brewing Trade in Scotland held in Edinburgh on Wednesday, at which I was not present, I was unanimously elected President of the combined associations. I shall have to find out what the duties are before I accept the position, but we may fairly take it as a compliment both to the company and myself.

'30 Mar: I note what you say about breaking new ground. Goodere is at present employed trying to find districts where there are still a fair number of free buyers left. They are a vanishing quantity. Even since you went into Parliament there is hardly a licence-holder dealing with us that dealt with us then. They have in great part entirely disappeared, having handed over their business to men in their employment or outside people, none of them having any money at all, who have been financed by brewers and are controlled accordingly. There are still a considerable number of free buyers in the Cardiff district, but the main drawback there is that the main consumption is a cheap mild ale sent out by the local brewers at from 20s. to 25s. per barrel.

'It is, no doubt, very disappointing that these big buyers whose trade we have recently purchased have done little more than arrest the shrinkage. I don't know if you have noticed that there is another very important factor working against us at present, and that is the reduced drinking habits of the people. An Official Return came out the other day showing that within the last few years the consumption of beer per head of the population had decreased from 32 gallons per annum to 27 gallons, and the paper went on to show that the shrinkage is still going on. We, however, see indications among our customers of an increasing consumption and, if the beer continues in its present excellent condition, we ought to do very well in the warm weather.

'5 April: Really the weather here is most exasperating, for after ten days of summer heat, we are back in winter again. While it will cool down that brisk beer, it will likely also check demand. While it goes without saying that the advantages of our open-air storage of beers are great and highly beneficial to the beer as well in any ordinary times, when we have a sudden change from mid-winter to real mid summer weather, without any intermediate stage, a lively beer like ours, sent out at the frozen point, will go fresh when subjected to a rise of some 20 degrees or more of temperature, and where cellars are exposed and management bad, in many cases it goes wild. That is what has been troubling us in Newcastle and district.

'16 April: The most important news today is that Henderson of South Shields, who has £40,000 on loan from us, has sold his business to a brewer in Durham called Johnson. The transaction is to be complete on the 1st July and that, I suppose, means we shall get our money back. Henderson in his letter says that Johnson will likely deal with us as he is a large buyer of Ritchie's (a rival Edinburgh brewer) at present. If we get the trade through Johnson without a loan it will be very good business for us, but even if we lose the trade we need not worry too much, because instead of £20,000 of pale ale per annum as he promised, Henderson has only taken since he started on 7 February 1906 £13,808 2s. worth of beer. During that period he has only returned £32 12s. 6d., being 2.5 per cent of his loan account. In addition to all that, he is a bad life. His heart is in a weak state and he recently quarrelled with his son for getting drunk on duty and turned him out of the place, so there is really no responsible person left to maintain the continuity of the business should anything happen to the old man.

'24 April: Mackay today reports what seems a particularly hard case in Dundee, where we have lost a customer who takes £1,000 in 12 months, whose licence has been taken away. You will remember a man Speed in Dundee, who owned one of the best houses there which he sold some years ago for £15,000, a transaction which made a great sensation at the time. Some years later it changed hands again at a much lower price and was ultimately bought by the present man, John Thomson, for £7,500. Well, last week a drunk man was found in the shop and for this, his first offence, the Justices have unanimously taken away the licence. Of course, he may get it back at the Appeal Court and if these facts which have been told Mackay are correct, he ought to, for it seems a monstrous thing to shut a house of that class up in this arbitrary way.

'29 April: There has been a very sharp rise in the barley market, caused by most unfavourable reports from both California and Asia Minor. Both countries are said to have been washed out by torrents of rain and the destruction is such that the crops will not amount to more than 50 per cent of a normal year. The prices of all available barleys have gone up accordingly. You will

McEwan's beer bottled at the brewery was exclusively for export. *Above*: bottling; *below*: making cases for bottles.

Wm Younger board meeting. Henry Johnston Younger is seated at the desk, his two sons on the right.

Younger's introduced the triple pyramid trade mark in 1859. With the addition of 'Co. Limited', this label is dated after the 1887 Companies Act.

understand the rise when I tell you that ordinary Danubian is now bringing 27s. Fortunately we are in a pretty strong position and at the Balance we shall carry over some 25,000 quarters of malt and barley.

'We are still in cold biting weather. There seems to be no end to the East wind this Spring.

'There has been a great deal of agitation going on in the trade over that Scottish Local Veto Bill, which got a second reading in the House on Thursday night. It does seem rather a scandal, although no member of the Government had a good word to say for that particular Bill, yet in the end all went and voted for it. But I don't suppose we shall hear anything more about it in this session.

'2 May: A poor man had his licence taken away the other day for no reason whatever against either himself or the house but simply because the Justices thought the district was a congested one. The poor man cried out that they might as well put their hand in his pocket and rob him, for he had put the savings of 25 years into the business and this decision had left him on the street, a ruined man. This harshness has caused a good deal of remark and if you look in today's *Scotsman*, you will see a description of what happened in Glasgow yesterday, where the feeling culminated in something like a riot at the Licensing Court, which got to such a pitch that the proposed Court had to be abandoned.

'I enclose the April sales, which show a fair increase, especially in Glasgow, and I hope we shall now move away in the West Country, which has been a dead weight for some time now. The military trade too is doing well, mainly caused by us having secured the Scots Greys at Piershill and the Seaforth Highlanders at the Castle.

'The blight on this sheet is the returns. This has been caused by the movements in the beer I have been telling you about, and it really is a black shame how publicans simply throw the beer back on our hands without any reason at all. The great bulk of them come bright in three days and brilliant in six, and it is enough to make a saint swear.

'4 May: We have had a characteristic letter from Alexander Deuchar today, demanding, not so much on behalf of himself, as he puts it, but on behalf of Reid and Higginbottom an extra 2.5 per cent discount. That group did £54,000 with us last year. You will remember we allowed them to group together as one buyer taking £50,000 and in consequence gave them 47.5 per cent. What angers me is that the disturbing element in this combination is that creature

Hop picking in Kent, 1900. *Clockwise from left*: delivery of filled hop sacks to an oast house; in the cooling loft; hop pickers 'tallying off'; and (at a merchant's warehouse) hop sampling.

A McEwan advertisement from 1906.

Higginbottom. The man only takes £5,900 and according to our scale he is only entitled to 37.5 per cent if he stood alone. A year ago he came here with the other two and did most of the talking until I rounded on him and took him firmly by the throat, with the result that he was glad to get out of the room. I don't feel exactly in the frame of mind to write to them temperately today and so I shall put off my refusal of the demand until Monday.

'8 May: You will be glad to hear that the Appeal Court in Dundee yesterday unanimously restored the licence to that house that used to belong to Speed. It seemed that the Justices in the Lower Court had been got at by the teetotallers. It really is a public scandal that the livelihood of decent people should be in the hands of such a contemptible lot.

'17 May: I last wrote on the 14th inst to Paris and I hope you have had a pleasant journey and arrived in London in good health. Deuchar continues to order as usual and, as he has never replied to my letter, I suppose for the time at least that fight is over.

'Harvey sent in a list the other day of about forty calls that he had made on houses in the Welsh valleys, where he had no success. He said there were only two free ones among them, so the state of the trade down there is much worse than we had supposed it to be.

'I don't know if you noticed the Beer Return, which came out the other day. It shows a very startling decline in the production of beer for the first three months of the year. During that period our sales showed an increase, and it would therefore seem that we are doing rather better than our neighbours.

'23 May: Our sales are rather better than last year and we have no complaints. Fermentation continues satisfactorily and the yeast is now up to the 150th turn.

'Maggie has just been here and I am going to lunch with her in the North British Hotel just now. There seems to have been some intolerable blundering about her rooms at the Caledonian Hotel this morning and she left the place, and no wonder. I am much annoyed that this should have happened and I shall see that those concerned are called to account for it. (As William McEwan was a large shareholder in both Caledonian and North British railways, this was no empty promise.)

'7 June: The last of our Californian barley came in today. The ship had made a very long voyage, but it is a magnificent delivery, far and away the best we have got this year. We bought ten thousand quarters, nine thousand at 26s. 6d. and one thousand at 27s. and the price they are asking today is over 30s. This is about 4s. above the price at this time last year and while it is possible we may be compelled to pay such prices, it would be folly to do it until we see more clearly that it is justified. So far I have not bought a bushel. Dealers blame heavy flooding and destruction of crops in Asia Minor and

Abbey & Holyrood Golf Club outing to Kilspindie, 1909.

'The progress of intemperance: tempted, persuaded, hardened, wrecked.' The temperance movement continued to give the brewing industry cause for considerable concern, as indicated by references in William McEwan's letters in this period.

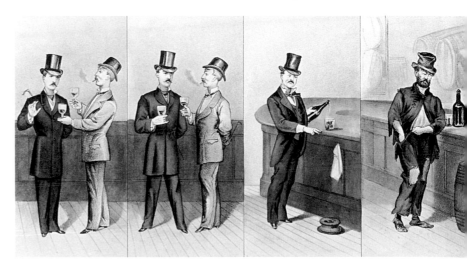

McEwan's, Duddingston and Deuchars labels of the late 19th – early 20th century. The Duddingston brewery was also operated by Robert Deuchar, which was later taken over by Newcastle Breweries.

California and the famine in Russia, but I am not altogether sure that the reports about California are true, and there is good reason to believe there is a heavy crop in Oregon.

'12 June: We are in pelting rain, to which there seems no end. I think I told you that we have been threatened with an increase of the Import Duty on beer into India. Some time ago a deputation of Indian brewers came to London and we got to hear they were very busy trying to nobble the Government on the ground that they were being unfairly treated by the competition from British brewers with large tied-house home trade which enabled them to dump their beer in India at under cost price. We heard they were being somewhat favoured by the Indian Office, so I wrote a letter pointing out that if their scheme was carried out it would discriminate against the British Troops in India, by whom the British beer was consumed, and said that 75 per cent of this beer was brewed in Scotland where there was little tied trade, so this claim was ridiculous. I wrote as chairman of the Brewers Association of Scotland and made the secretary sign it too. We have now got a letter from the India Office saying my letter has been forwarded to the Government of India, so it would appear that we have spiked the guns of these Indian brewers. Of course, we have not very much of that Indian trade at present, but now that the late restrictions are to be rescinded at the end of the year and commanding officers are allowed to make their own arrangements, we expect a fair share.

I am, yours affectionately, Wm Younger.'

To the satisfaction of even the Scottish brewers, the 1907 Licensing Bill provoked strong opposition, with protest meetings across England and hundreds of letters to MPs. The Liberal Government lost several by-elections by massive margins and a rally organised by the drinks industry in Hyde Park in September 1908, was attended by half a million, many travelling into London on special trains. Bowing to the inevitable, the Government withdrew the Bill, but took its revenge by increasing the cost of licences from a maximum of £60 a year to several hundreds for large public houses. London pubs were especially affected and the big brewers were forced to put up the price of beer for the first time for almost a hundred years, from 4*d*. to 5*d*. a quart. The Lords rejected the Budget, and the price dropped back again, but this did nothing to improve profit margins. By 1911, Younger's had written close to £100,000 off its London loans.

In spite of these losses, though, the company was still investing in public houses in greater London and the North-East. This was largely because the licensees had gone broke owing it money, usually in the form of first or second mortgages. But it could afford to take a long view. Although the trend in profits from the peak of £132,000 in 1898 had been resolutely downwards, they were still averaging around £90,000 a year. And Younger's possessed large cash reserves – like most of its Scottish competitors, it had always believed in putting more than a little aside.

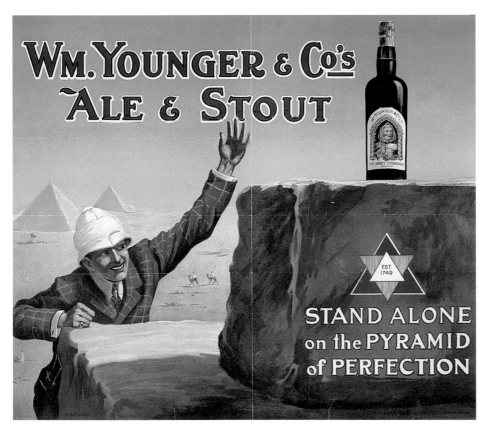

This poster of 1909 shows a British tourist scaling a pyramid to find his 'prize' on the peak. The interlocking triangles of Younger's trade mark happily reflect the pyramid motif.

It was not all bad news. Higher duty on spirits boosted sales of beer in 1911, as did a splendid summer. Business improved again the following year, in spite of a coal strike in the North-East, a dock strike in the Port of London, the price of hops doubling, barley and casks costing more, wages rising and a cold, wet July and August.

But the shadow of war with Germany hung over the future. Younger's had been paying a 10s. a week allowance to employees training for the Territorial Army since June 1909. And when the company bought its first lorry from Halley's Industrial Motors for £560 in February 1912, the War Office provided a £15-a-year subsidy in return for the right to borrow it for manoeuvres.

Henry Younger died in March 1913, at the age of 81. William McEwan's death, aged 85, came two months later. The King and Queen sent a message of condolence to his family and a service of remembrance was held in Edinburgh. An era had ended.

There were hundreds of demonstrations against licensing laws in 1908 – this one in Hyde Park, London.

The Blue Bell, Eaglescliff, Stockton-on-Tees. The original deeds for the premises are dated 1753, when it was already a pub. Its riverside location has been the focus of several dramatic episodes in its history, including a bloody skirmish during the Civil War of the 1640s on Yarm Bridge, within view of the pub.

8

All Ends Up

The drinks industry throughout Great Britain and Ireland was severely affected by the Great War. Apart from the recruitment of most of their employees into the armed forces, brewers faced large increases in taxation, drastic reductions in the supply and rises in the price of raw materials, and unheard of restrictions on the sale of alcoholic drinks.

Scotland was as badly hit as the rest of the UK. During 1913, Scottish beer production had reached nearly 2m. barrels. It was to prove an all-time record. By 1916, output had fallen by 25 per cent and the following two years saw it drop to less than 900,000 barrels in 1917 and little more than 700,000 barrels in 1918.

The early months of the war, however, gave little hint of the privations to come. Firms like Younger's and McEwan's, with links to Scottish and English regiments stretching back for half a century, worked 24 hours a day to meet orders for the British forces in France. Incautiously, a large consignment of Younger's bottled beer was put in a London provisions store which had a glass roof. The summer of 1915 was notoriously hot, hundreds of corks popped out and beer flooded over the food on the lower floors. Men were rushed south from the Abbey Brewery to mop up the precious liquid. It took them two months, but they salvaged 75 per cent. Heaven knows what it tasted like.

Demand remained strong, in spite of large increases in duty, but the brewery industry's ability to supply it was soon curtailed by the Government, largely to reduce drinking around military and naval bases, and in the armaments and shipbuilding industries. 'Drink is doing us more

Workers at Newcastle's Haymarket Brewery before the Great War.

McEwan's fire brigade, c.1910. Half the men worked by day and the other half by night.

damage than all the German submarines put together,' the new Minister of Munitions, David Lloyd George, remarked in February 1915. A Central Control Board was created the following July, under the Defence of the Realm Act, which immediately limited licensing hours in strategic areas where drunkenness was a major problem. Opening hours were restricted to two hours in the middle of the day, from noon to 2 p.m., and three in the evening, from 6 p.m. to 9 p.m. In particularly sensitive areas, such as Gretna, where a huge national munitions complex was being built out of range of German aircraft, and Invergordon and Cromarty, where quiet fishing villages were being transformed into a major naval base for the Home Fleet, the Central Control Board took direct control of all public houses, closing many and insisting on major improvements to those that remained.

The initial effect of the restrictions was simply to create problems elsewhere. Hordes of thirsty labourers at Gretna, for example, descended on Carlisle, just over the border in England, where 'scenes of the most nauseating and degrading character became a common occurrence,' according to one observer. 'Men fought like beasts, fierce fights raged round the doors of public houses . . . and almost every alley was littered with prostrate drunken men.' The Control Board responded by extending State ownership north and south of Gretna. By the end of 1916, five breweries in Carlisle and Maryport and all the pubs on either side of the Solway Firth, an area of 500 sq. miles, had been taken over.

Scottish brewers responded opportunistically to the new situation. In September 1915, for example, McEwan's quoted a Glasgow wholesaler to Gretna 30s. a barrel for canteen beer, with a specific gravity of 1045 degrees, and 36s. a barrel for canteen stout, at 1065 degrees, less a 5 per cent

discount for monthly payment. The price did not include a War Tax surcharge of 16*s.* 6*d.* per barrel on the beer and 22*s.* 6*d.* on the stronger stout. 'We make a speciality of this canteen beer,' William Younger wrote. 'It is full bodied, has a fine flavour and yet is very light in alcohol, which combination suits the tastes of the men and meets the views of the commanding officers. We may further mention that the same beer and stout has been given preference by the War Office for shipment to the Dardanelles, we having despatched there within the last two weeks 2,000 barrels of the former and 500 barrels of the latter.'

Similar restrictions were imposed around the Tyne, Wear and Tees, to preserve productivity in the shipbuilding industry. Only a dozen of Newcastle Breweries' pubs fell outside the area taken over by the Central Control Board and Thomas Lovibond warned shareholders that the next few years would be difficult. It was an accurate prediction. The price of hops and malt doubled, and in 1916 all breweries were ordered by Customs and Excise to reduce output to 70 per cent of their pre-war total.

Inevitably, too, exports fell as troops were brought home from the colonies and merchant ships were commandeered to supply the UK. Margins on the few shipments allowed were limited by exorbitant freight rates and high insurance premiums to cover war risks. The Easter Rising in Ireland in 1916 further restricted Younger's business.

The brewing industry was also hard hit by conscription. By March 1916, only three men of military age were still working at McEwan's Fountain Brewery. More than 200 men had joined the armed forces and their places had been taken by 'over 100 women, old men, Italians male and female, niggers and what not'. Half the company's office staff had also left for the front, leaving their jobs to women, boys and old soldiers. Pleas for exemption or postponement for essential staff went largely unheard.

The Scottish brewers reacted to restrictions on production by an agreement not to compete with each other for customers. It was a difficult arrangement to police. In April 1916, Younger's accused McEwan's of poaching some of its Glasgow trade. McEwan's replied firmly that if this was so, it was none of its seeking. It admitted that its Glasgow trade had grown considerably, but only as a result of a direct approach from a combination of buyers, many of them previously customers of another Edinburgh brewery, Muir's, which had just closed down. 'We offered them 40 per cent discount and 2.5 per cent for cash, with a further 2.5 per cent if the total trade reached a certain figure, (which) has now been reached. We have no knowledge of your discounts, nor did we know, indeed, that these men were your customers at all. In view of these facts, we think you will admit that there has been no contravention on our part of the letter or the spirit of the agreement.'

Tax bore heavily on all companies. McEwan's found itself in trouble with the Inland Revenue over a £15,000 reserve fund to maintain dividends in bad years. Its chairman and managing director, William Younger, revealed

'Drink is doing us more damage than all the German submarines put together,' according to Minister of Munitions David Lloyd George, shown here at the Front in February 1915.

The head office of Gretna munitions complex. The Government took direct control of public houses in the area in an attempt to limit alcohol consumption.

1916 recruitment poster by
Alfred Leete, creator of the
famous Younger's 'Father
William', who first appeared
in 1921.

Barras Reed returned from the
War to became chairman of
Newcastle Breweries in 1918.

to Edinburgh's Inspector of Taxes that the fund had been in existence ever since the company went public, and admitted that it was not generally known to the staff.

In February 1917, the Government banned the manufacture of new malt. And in May, it commandeered all stocks of unmalted barley. Great Britain was literally on the bread line. The country's situation was becoming desperate, with widespread industrial unrest mirroring near-mutiny in the armed forces. The death toll was appalling. Of the 400 employees of Younger's who served their country in the Great War, 74 died, including the company's youngest director, Andrew Smith's nephew Arthur Ferguson, who was killed in action in October 1917.

The ban on malt in February was accompanied by another 15 per cent reduction in beer output. Newcastle Breweries was forced to close all its pubs on Mondays and 'at any other time thought appropriate'. Thomas Lovibond, as president of the Institute of Brewing, joined an industry delegation to the Prime Minister pleading for relief. The limit on production was relaxed during the three summer months and, with beer prices up, Younger's, astonishingly, achieved a record profit in 1917 of £138,735. Comparable results were reported by many breweries. But the figures were an illusion. The value of the pound had fallen by a third since the beginning of the war and Younger's earnings were, in any case, before much higher rates of tax. Even so, the industry's performance was good enough to prompt the Government to double beer duty to 50s. a barrel in April 1918. Newcastle Breweries, already charging 4d. a pint for ale down to a gravity of 1025 degrees, had no choice but to put up its prices yet again. To the working people of Newcastle, faced with such serious food shortages that rationing had been introduced, it was almost the last straw. Exhausted and overworked, Thomas Lovibond died a few months later, aged 70. Barras Reed took his place as chairman.

The end of the war sparked a brief boom, fuelled by rising prices, the release of wartime profits by many companies in the form of free shares and bonuses to employees, and a widespread belief that everything would return to pre-war conditions. Heavy investment took place in industries such as shipbuilding, where the tonnage under construction rose by 50 per cent in two years. But the brewing industry found the change to peacetime conditions very difficult. Barley and hops were expensive and the Government was ungenerous, raising beer duty to 70s. a barrel in 1919 and to 100s. a barrel in 1920.

Newcastle Breweries also found itself embroiled in another legal action, this time against the Admiralty. In 1917, the Navy Board had requisitioned 239 puncheons of rum from the company, for which it had only offered to pay the cost of buying it from the West Indies. Newcastle Breweries, with the backing of other firms which had been similarly treated, argued that compensation for the rum should include the expense of blending and storage, plus the difference between the original price and the much higher current cost of replacing it, thanks to the fall in the value of sterling. The High Court ruled in Newcastle Breweries' favour in 1920, but before it could collect, the Government passed an Indemnity Act which meant the company had to resubmit its claim to a new War Compensation Court. This took two more years. Three years later, the Inland Revenue claimed that the compensation the brewery had finally received amounted to a trading profit made in 1918, and was therefore liable to excess profits tax of 80 per cent.

But its difficulties did not prevent Newcastle Breweries extending the Tyne Brewery, adding to the Northern Corporation's portfolio of public houses, and taking over two more local businesses, the South Shields brewery of Matthew Wood & Sons, which was reputed to have been founded in 1750, and Newcastle wine merchants Turnbull & Wood. Plans were made to extend the bottling plant in Bath Lane and the company's assistant brewer, James Porter, and its chief chemist, Archie Jones, began experimenting with a premium brown ale to suit local tastes. 'We tried for a long time all ends up,' Porter admitted later. 'We wanted something different but not too strong. No one was allowed to mention what was going on, but we varied it so much that few really knew.'

Scottish brewers also did well. In 1920, in spite of high costs and raising wages twice in the year,

The end of the War sparked a brief economic boom in the UK. The Government raised beer duty to 70s. a barrel in 1919 and to 100s. a barrel in 1920.

Left to right: Louis Fletcher, John Mantell and J. Spiers in the Water Analysis Room of the Holyrood laboratory, c.1920.

Bottling girls, Newcastle. Manpower shortages during the War started what was no longer seen as unusual by 1928 – women doing what had previously been regarded as men's jobs.

'Wild oats!' by Peter Frazer. Detail from a William Younger advertisement, probably 1920s.

WILD OATS !

Younger's could afford to invest in new plant at Holyrood for bottling chilled and carbonated beer, and pay its ordinary shareholders a special bonus of £225,000, out of its cash reserves, which had grown to an embarrassing £600,000. It spent a fraction of them on a library for its staff in Holyrood Brewery, built a bowling green in the grounds of its Moray Park maltings, and took its employees on two or even three day annual outings, some as far afield as London and Belfast.

The post-war boom was abruptly ended by an attack on inflation in the form of higher interest rates, triggering a sustained fall in prices and a frightening rise in unemployment, which doubled in the winter of 1920/21 to almost two million. Coal mining was exceptionally badly affected, with production dropping by 40m. tons from its pre-war level of 280m. tons, mostly due to a two-thirds decline in exports as European mines came back into production. Reductions in wages and jobs led to regional strikes, even though the industry was still under government control. Worse was to come. When Lloyd George gave the coal mines back to their pre-war owners at the end of March 1921, they immediately locked out every miner who would not accept a drastic cut in pay. In some areas, the reductions were nearly 50 per cent.

The strike that followed resulted in a bitter defeat for the miners and a general collapse in resistance to lower earnings. By the end of 1922, manufacturing wages in most of the UK were down by around 40 per cent. It was not such a savage deal as might appear, as prices had fallen almost as fast, with the cost of living index declining by 35 per cent between 1920 and 1922. But the situation was much worse in parts of Scotland and the north-east of England, where the demise of shipbuilding and the munitions industry deprived whole communities of work.

The brewers were also worried by a revival of the temperance movement, inspired by the Eighteenth Amendment to the US Constitution, which prohibited the manufacture and sale of alcohol throughout the USA in 1920. This coincided with the first local polls in Scotland under the 1913 Temperance (Scotland) Act, which produced enough success for the prohibition factor to cause concern. Edwin Scrymgeour, the founder of the Scottish Prohibition Party, defeated Winston Churchill at Dundee in the 1922 General Election. But the drinks industry did not lack seasoned campaigners in its defence. Archie Younger was a veteran, speaking at licensed trade functions across the UK against the series of liquor control bills introduced in both Houses of Parliament. Inveighing against the Bishop of Liverpool's 1926 Liquor Popular Control Bill, he told the Leicestershire Licensed Victuallers' Protection and Benevolent Association that the initial successes of the prohibitionists in Scotland were gradually being taken back from them. Since 1920, 25 'dry' areas had reverted to the old licence system, and a poll in 1926 showed 236,000 votes against prohibition, compared to 150,000 in favour.

Anti-temperance cartoon: 'Escaped with loss of a feather or two.' The prohibitionist Pussyfoot just fails to destroy the Personal Freedom of the average drinker in Scotland.

Brewers responded to pressure from the temperance movement and tax increases by raising standards in public houses.

'Father William' by Charles Folkard for a
later edition of Lewis Carroll's *Alice in
Wonderland*.

Younger's Father William first appeared in
a press advertisement in 1921. The artist
was Alfred Leete, the creator of the famous
wartime Kitchener poster, *page 86*.

Early unsigned sketch of
Younger's Father William.

The prohibitionists might be failing in their prime objective, but they did
reflect widespread concern about drink and drinking. Although perhaps the
main cause of a fall in consumption in 1920 was the high price of a pint,
thanks to the seventh successive rise in beer duty to £5 a barrel. The
brewers responded by raising standards in their public houses and
promoting new products. Younger's 'Father William', plagiarised from Lewis
Carroll's poem in *Alice in Wonderland*, first appeared in a press
advertisement in 1921, over the couplet:

'You are old, Father William, the young man did say,
All nonsense my lad, I get YOUNGER each day.'

The artist was Alfred Leete, the creator of the famous wartime poster
portraying Lord Kitchener with an outstretched finger over the caption: Your
Country Needs You. 'Father William' was registered as a trademark in 1927

and Leete drew him for Younger's until his death in 1933. The copyright was bought from his widow for £175 the following year. The character was first used to label Younger's sparkling Holyrood Ale, bottled in the company's new plant. But during the next twenty years 'Father William' was to appear on Abbey Ale, Best Pale Ale and Old Scotch Stout. And he survives in various guises today.

Just as successful, though, was Younger's Scotch Ale, which continued to attract a devoted clientele, especially in London, where fresh houses were acquired and refurbished in a distinctive mock-Tudor style, as were the existing pubs in the City and the West End. Substantial sums were also spent on rebuilding and improving Younger's chain of pubs in the North-East. By the standards of the day, Younger's senior managers Robert Bruce jnr, George Stenhouse's son Alistair ('Ally') and Harry Younger's son John William ('Jock'), were enthusiastic modernisers. Giving evidence to the Scottish Licensing Commission in Edinburgh as president of the Brewers Association of Scotland, Bruce said that he thought any improvements to public houses that promoted social intercourse should be encouraged. He added daringly that he would like to see music and games allowed.

A reduction in duty of 24s. a barrel brought the price of beer down by 1d. a pint in 1924, and the abolition of hop controls by the new

An advertising design at the rough stage, probably from the 1940s.

A 1950s advertisement, reused as a Christmas card in the 1980s.

The oldest existing bottle of
Newcastle Brown Ale, 1927.

Entirely New

YOU have tasted nothing *quite* the same as this before . . . a good Brown Ale with a rich mellow flavour, recalling the famous "Audit" Ales of bygone days.

It's just the right strength . . . not too heavy for summer drinking, yet with sufficient "body" to satisfy the man who likes a good Ale, and knows when he gets it.

Let your own good judgment tell you how excellent Newcastle BROWN Ale really is. Test it for yourself . . . try a bottle to-night.

Newcastle Brown ALE

The right strength . . the right flavour.

Imperial Pint Bottles	9/- per dozen.
Imperial Half-Pints	5/- per dozen.

BREWED BY THE NEWCASTLE BREWERIES LTD.

The first Newcastle Brown Ale
advertisement appeared in 1927.

Conservative Government the following year removed another burden on the industry. But economic conditions in the north of England continued to decline following Winston Churchill's decision, as Chancellor of the Exchequer, to restore sterling to its pre-war value by returning the UK to the Gold Standard. The result was a flood of cheap imports, including coal from Germany. The owners of the UK coal industry promptly reneged on the minimum pay agreement they had imposed the year before. The miners reacted furiously and the Trades Union Council supported their demand for 'not a penny off the pay, not a second on the day'. On 4 May 1926, over one and a half million workers in the building, chemical, iron and steel, power, printing and transport industries came out on strike across the whole of the UK in support of one million coal miners locked out of their jobs. They stayed out for nine days, partially paralysing the economy, until the TUC privately conceded defeat and called off the action. The direct impact of the General Strike on industrial relations generally was small and on the coal mining dispute non-existent, with the stubborn miners remaining locked out by their equally intransigent bosses until November.

For a brief period, though, the country appeared to be on the brink of anarchy. On Tyneside, public houses closed at 9 p.m. and Newcastle Breweries took out insurance against riot damage. And the company's lorry drivers obeyed the Transport Workers Federation's call to strike, which stranded deliveries of beer in the brewery. The *Brewing Trade Review* reported that one of the deprived customers was a local miners' club, which sent some of its members to collect its order. As they left the brewery, they were stopped by the TWF picket. 'Well,' said one of the striking drivers. 'This is the limit. Here are we chaps losing a week's pay to come out on strike on your behalf, and you have the cheek to come and do our jobs for us!' Or words to that effect.

In spite of the strike and the continuing recession, sales remained buoyant enough to launch Newcastle Brown Ale at a premium price of 9s. for a dozen pint bottles. By then Porter and Jones had radically improved all the brewery's manufacturing processes. At the Brewers Exhibition in London the following year, the company won the *Brewers' Journal* Challenge Cup for the best draught beer, the *Brewing Trade Review* Cup for the best bottled beer, a gold medal for the best light bitter, and four other prizes. It was the most impressive performance by any brewery in the exhibition's 40-year history. James Porter was made head brewer in 1929.

SCOTTISH & NEWCASTLE
PUBS TODAY

The King's Head, in the small market town of Masham, on the River Ure, by the Yorkshire Dales, was built in the second half of the 18th century. In addition to its principal function it was at one time, surprisingly, an excise office, as well as a posting house.

9

A Force for Temperance

Early in December 1930, Younger's and McEwan's surprised the Scottish brewing industry by announcing that they had 'negotiated a combination of certain of their financial and technical resources with a view of further developing the efficiency of the production and distribution of their ales.'

It was evidence of how deeply the seemingly endless recession was biting. Both companies were still profitable, but the future looked blacker than ever. Unemployment had risen above two million and margins were being squeezed by another rise in duty; only 3s. a barrel, but the Labour Chancellor of the Exchequer, Philip Snowden, had made the brewers promise not to pass the extra tax onto consumers in the price they charged for their beer.

The formal announcement of the new combine on 5 December stated that each company would continue to be managed as a separate business. Scottish Brewers, as the new holding company was to be called, was very much an arm's-length organisation, with the directors of the operating companies jealously guarding their autonomy.

On paper, Younger's was the dominant partner, with its shareholders acquiring approximately two-thirds of the equity of Scottish Brewers. This was a reflection of the relative value of the two companies. Younger's assets at the time of the merger were valued at £2.25m., against the figure of just under £1.5m. put on McEwan's. To a certain extent, McEwan's growth had slackened after the First World War. William Younger had retired and the company was chaired by an accountant, Eric Beilby. Exaggeratedly, Harry Younger described the Fountain Brewery as 'practically derelict'. But

SCOTTISH & NEWCASTLE PUBS TODAY

The Black Lion, Hammersmith. A pub has stood here on the bank of the River Thames for at least two centuries. In the bar hangs a portrait of Alan Herbert, author of witty poetry and musicals, one of the many celebrated artists, authors and actors who have frequented the pub over the years.

Harry George Younger, chairman
of Youngers and Scottish Brewers
1913–51.

'A Tavern in Bloomsbury' by
William Grant, 1929. Younger's
assets were greater than
McEwan's, in part because of the
value of its London pubs.

McEwan's bottling plant, with its glass-lined storage tanks and modern
carbonating and filtering equipment, was among the most up-to-date in the
country. However, the division also recognised the worth of Younger's
portfolio of English pubs.

On the other hand, McEwan's had won a far greater share of the UK's
export and military markets. This was recognised by the formation of a
separate company named McEwan-Younger to handle all military and naval
contracts, and overseas business. Both breweries would provide their beer
to the new sales company at cost, and 75 per cent of the profits made by
McEwan-Younger would go to McEwan's. Younger's store at the Army's vast
camp at Catterick in Yorkshire was closed down and its business transferred
to McEwan's larger operation there. Other developments included a decision
to sell some redundant premises in Malta, an approach to Jardine Matheson
to ask if the Hong Kong-based trading group would like to share in the cost
of building a new bottling plant in Shanghai, and plans for a price war in
the West Indies against recent competition from Tennents and Jeffreys:

'Demerara. We make arrangements to ship from our large stock of McEwan
brand stout whatever quantities are necessary, a new label being employed
for the purpose bearing McEwan-Younger's name. To commence with this,
stout will be placed on the market at $1 below the present rates ruling for
Jeffrey and Tennent. "M" and "Y" brands will be retained on the market at
current prices, but sales will be more or less negligible during this campaign.
Every effort to be made to secure as large a turnover as possible with the
object of getting Jeffrey and Tennent to reduce their
prices. When that is achieved we can drop our prices still
further and just ship on a sufficient scale to ensure that
Jeffrey's and Tennent's prices come down also. This policy
can be continued as long as necessary . . . to bring home
forcibly to both Messrs. Jeffrey and Tennent that we are
not prepared to stand aside and see our trade crippled in
other profitable markets.

'Jamaica. Every effort to be made to protect our existing
trade, which has always been very valuable as far as "M"
brand is concerned . . . Jeffrey's inroads in Jamaica have
until recently been confined to their Pilsener beer, but
these last few months they are now making inroads into
the stout and strong ale trade. The best prospect of
protecting our strong ale and stout trade (seems to be) by
breaking the monopoly Jeffrey have secured for their
Pilsener beer. As a matter of fact, our Pale Ale has practically disappeared from this market. It is proposed to allot
the sum of £1,000 to be expended in Jamaica this year on
advertising and propaganda work. More than likely the
major portion of this sum will be spent on pushing
Pilsener beer. The retail price of all brands is more or less

the same, the wholesale and retail merchants pocketing the difference which in many instances amounts to a good few shillings per case. It would seem therefore that we should endeavour to make a direct appeal to the consumer with the object of getting him to demand "M" and "Y" brands.'

No record survives of the outcome of this campaign, which was conducted during 1932. Nor of the success of a cheap bottled beer, delivered under a 'neutral' label at a price of 17s. per case to India's main ports, and aimed at the bazaar markets in the same year. But a hint appeared in the minutes of Scottish Brewers early in 1934 that the price war was proving painful. A letter from McEwan-Younger suggested that a reduction in the prices it was currently paying of one-third of one penny for each degree of gravity would considerably ease matters, in view of the difficulties imposed by the rising cost of beer on its operations. The main board directors agreed to recommend the concession to the operating companies. But the relationship worked both ways. Two years later, McEwan's had to raise its price to McEwan-Younger by 1s. a barrel to cover higher than expected production costs. Younger's price was put up by the same amount.

Liaison between the two companies was gradually increasing. One of the bridges was a joint advertising committee, which held its first meeting in April 1932, chaired by Harry Younger's son Harry Johnston. The committee began by comparing the 1931 advertising budgets of both companies. Younger's was revealed to have spent £31,000 the previous year, of which £17,000 had been in London, against McEwan's total of £15,000. A major cost for each company had been press advertisements, but considerable sums had been invested in promotional material for pubs, such as showcards, service trays, rubber mats, tobacco pouches, book matches, bottle openers and ashtrays. In McEwan's case, the biggest expenditure had been on football fixture books, which the company distributed in huge quantities. A suggestion that McEwan's might cut down on this outlay in future stumbled over the fact that an order had already been placed for the forthcoming season.

But the committee soon got into its stride, choosing new advertising agents and discussing the need for a central figure for McEwan's advertisements comparable with Younger's 'Father William'. McEwan's new agency came up with 'The McEwan Man', a rather uninspired figure which it suggested could be put on badges in the colours of Scottish football teams. An order was placed for 250,000 badges, but this was sharply reduced after fears were expressed that their distribution in Glasgow might provoke confrontations between fans. 'The McEwan Man' gave way to a small boy wearing a Tam o' Shanter, scarf and apron. Designed by Bert Thomas, he was

McEwan ashtray. Considerable sums were invested during the 1930s to promote the brand image in pubs.

Wm Younger's showcard. In the 1930s there was no Advertising Standards Authority to contest Father William's claim.

Just what the Doctor ordered!

Wm YOUNGER'S

Scotch Ale

One of the first posters in a campaign collectively funded by all brewers as a remedy for the effects of the Great Depression. Nationwide sales had dropped by 34 per cent (24.6m. to 17.9m. barrels) between 1929 and 1933. The campaign ran for almost 40 years.

Ramsay MacDonald (bottom) with members of coalition cabinet, 1931. Duty on beer rose by 31s. a barrel in the new government's first budget.

christened 'The Wee McEwan'. The day after his first appearance in the Press, full-page adverts were run by a rival Edinburgh brewer, William Murray, depicting a small boy in a Tam o' Shanter, scarf and kilt, under the wording 'The Original Wee Murray'. Harry J. hastily explained to Murray's managing director that McEwan's had been honestly ignorant of the existence of the rival character and agreed to change 'Wee' to 'Willie' and swap the apron for long trousers. Sadly, the public did not find 'Willie McEwan' any more attractive than 'The McEwan Man' and the company was forced to fall back on a variation of the slogan being used by the current national beer advertising campaign, 'Beer is Best'. More successful ideas included McEwan's Cavalier, first pictured on hanging lamps, neon pub signs and branded watches. In 1937, McEwan's ordered 300,000 pencils, costing £800, to mark the coronation of King George VI. Younger's settled for book matches.

Other examples of co-operation between the two companies were joint bids for public houses at an auction of a Leeds brewery named Haughton & Reed, a loan from McEwan's to Younger's in the spring of 1934 when the latter was a little short of cash, and combined pressure on the London, Midland & Scottish Railway to increase its orders of McEwan's beer in recognition of the large volume of both companies' products it was carrying as freight. More significantly, in May 1936, Younger's and McEwan's agreed to merge their malting departments as a separate subsidiary of Scottish Brewers.

But in most respects the two companies went their separate ways. The early days of the partnership coincided with one of the most frightening periods in British economic history, with a coalition Government led by Ramsay MacDonald declaring a National Emergency and, among other panic measures, raising beer duty by 31s. a barrel. Predictably, this led to a sharp fall in consumption. The Gold Standard was also abandoned. Happily, the devaluation of sterling helped melt the economic permafrost that had gripped the country for so long. Beer margins remained tight, but sales began to improve and confidence in the future recovered enough in 1932 for Younger's to invest in spacious new London premises at Princes Wharf in Lambeth, facing across the Thames towards Somerset House downstream from Waterloo Bridge. Archie Younger, Younger's vice-chairman, and William Bond, its London manager, were given handsomely panelled offices, the staff was provided with a canteen and a recreation room, one floor was shared with McEwan-Younger, and a large garage housed the company's fleet of 4-ton lorries. All Younger's business in the south of England was supplied from its London stores, which still received most of their stocks by sea. Twice a week ships from Leith made a 36-hour voyage to the docks below Tower Bridge, where 1,500 barrels at a time were unloaded into barges and transported up river to Princes Wharf. There they were rolled down ramps which ran all the way into Younger's new store.

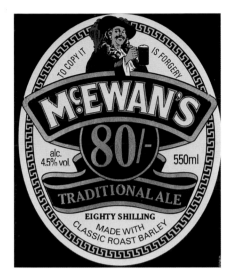

The McEwan's cavalier, seen here on a 1990s beer label, has been in use since the success of the poster series, *left*, which first appeared in the late 1930s.

McEwan-Younger export labels for the Far East, glamourising light beers by associating them with the elegant comedies and swashbuckling romances that the Hollywood film industry had made so successful in the 1930s.

The following year Younger's bought the Collin Croft brewery at Kendal, following the death of its owner, who had been the company's agent in the Lake District. Younger's opened a bottling plant at Collin Croft; demand expanded so rapidly that within four years a larger bottling hall was needed. The Kendal brewery also became the focus for further expansion of Younger's chain of public houses. And more money was invested in improvements to the existing portfolio.

McEwan-Younger's export label
for Rangoon, Burma.

Edward Reed, 1941.

Newcastle Breweries had a tougher time. Since 1927, the company had been managed by Barras Reed's son Edward. The north-east of England remained one of the worst affected regions of the UK. By 1932, many collieries were closed, no ships were being built on Tyneside, more than a hundred vessels lay idle at moorings, and a quarter of a million men were out of work between Blyth and the Tees. Newcastle Breweries cut salaries and failed to pay a dividend for the first time in its history. Once the crisis was over, however, Edward Reed began to upgrade the group's licensed premises.

Reed was a strong believer in the need for better pubs. 'Had I been a social worker thirty years ago, I might easily now be sitting on the Licensing Bench as a staunch teetotaller,' he told members of the Newcastle and Gateshead Licensed Victuallers Association at their annual dinner in the County Hall in 1938. 'I am perfectly certain that the behaviour of the public in the past and a good deal of laxity in the running of all this trade are primarily responsible for all the restrictions under which we suffer today. That being so, it is obvious that the remedy is for this trade to be so well run that it can become the most potent force operating for temperance in the whole country.'

A full-page advertisement feature in the *Tyneside Industrial Review* reported that Newcastle Breweries had decided in 1931 that a complete programme of rebuilding and renovation must be carried out, 'whatever the cost'. Many pubs were pulled down and rebuilt to cater for the more affluent, car-owning customers that were appearing in ever greater numbers even in the stricken North-East. Newcastle Breweries did its best to retain features of architectural and historical interest, but most of its new pubs were model 'road-houses', spacious, neoclassical brick buildings with imposing porticos, such as the Duke of Wellington in Kenton Lane, Newcastle.

Brian Bennison and James Merrington, in their history of Newcastle Breweries from 1890 to 1990, described this as built to a basic plan, with central services and lavatories on the ground floor surrounded by a select room, a sitting room, a bar and a 'men only' buffet. A stairway led from a main hallway to a first-floor lounge big enough to accommodate 240 people, as well as an orchestra which occasionally broadcast on local radio; both were paved in vitreous mosaic featuring the company's Blue Star trademark (conceived by Edward Reed in 1934, the star's five points notionally commemorated Newcastle Breweries' five founding companies). Burnt-glass scenes from the Battle of Waterloo decorated the stairwell and pictures from Edward Reed's own collection, including two original letters signed by Wellington, hung in the rooms. At the rear, a colonnaded balcony strung with fairy-lights overlooked a seven-rink bowling green set in 42 acres.

Attention to detail extended to inn signs. The wrought-iron sign for the Angler's Arms at Weldon Bridge in Northumberland was designed by Edward Reed himself. It survives today, as a gate in Gavin Reed's garden.

By 1938, Reed's improvement programme was virtually complete. It had included shedding some of the group's smaller and less profitable pubs, as well as buying a few larger houses, such as the White Horse Hotel in Newcastle's Groat Market and the Royal Hotel, Hexham. Demand for beer picked up so much that the Tyne Brewery had to extend its malt milling and bottling departments. In 1938, production was a new record. How much this was due to better pubs and how much to the revival in industrial activity in the region was a moot point.

The recovery was fuelled by rearmament. Mass production of gas masks began as early as 1936. Two years later, the first of Newcastle Breweries' employees were called up. Others of military age were encouraged to join the Territorial Army and special leave was granted for training.

Scottish Brewers made similar arrangements. The industry had just agreed to give its workers a week's paid holiday a year. Territorials and reservists called up for a month's training were offered an additional week on full pay while they were in camp, plus two weeks with full pay less Army pay.

Now a gate in Gavin Reed's garden, an inn sign designed by Edward Reed for the Angler's Arms, Weldon Bridge, Northumberland.

Centre: Newcastle Breweries made plans to protect its employees in anticipation of air raids.

'Own label' beer label for India International of Bombay. One of many supplied to the tropics by McEwan-Younger.

Clerical staff did better. They got full pay for the entire month and a fortnight's paid holiday as well. The Scottish brewing industry also struck a deal with the Transport & General Workers Union for a two-year pay freeze. In principle, this included apprentices and women employees.

A committee met to consider how to protect employees during air raids. Plans were drawn up to build shelters and organise their use. The board of Scottish Brewers approved the expenditure of £300 on sandbags, gas masks, blankets and electric torches. However, it also began to worry about essential supplies such as barley, hops and beer barrels. Robert Bruce warned that not only was a shortage of timber likely, but many casks sent abroad might not be returned. Younger's and McEwan's were advised to buy what barrels and barrel-making material they could lay their hands on. The sudden, unceremonious return home of the British Army from the beaches of Dunkirk reduced demand from mainland Europe, but German submarines made sure that UK timber imports were minimal. When William Lindsay & Son's cooperage in Canonmills came up for sale in 1942 at a price of £83,000, Scottish Brewers snapped it up.

In contrast to the previous war, 'temperance' was out of favour. MP Quintin Hogg argued bluntly, 'Beer is the innocent pleasure of many millions, especially those who bear the brunt today.'

Right: a few of those who bore the brunt indulging in some 'innocent pleasure'.

Facing page: 'To set a man up for the winter', another example from the beer industry's collective advertising campaign.

The Second World War, however, did not affect Scottish Brewers or Newcastle Breweries anything like as severely as the First. Admittedly tax on beer shot up, pushing the price of a pint from 5*d.* to 1*s.* by 1941. And Bruce's fears about shortages were fulfilled. There were no imports of barley, supplies of sugar were reduced by 40 per cent and of hops by 20 per cent. But relations between the industry and the Government were much better, with the Brewers' Society working closely with the Ministry of Food on the distribution and rationing of many supplies. And the temperance movement's call for restrictions on drinking, under the slogan 'Alcohol, A Foe to Britain', fell on unsympathetic ears. 'The Temperance Council must clearly understand that the national emergency is not a moment to introduce temperance propaganda under the cloak of national necessity,' Quintin Hogg, MP for Oxford, said bluntly. 'Beer is the innocent pleasure of many millions, especially those who bear the brunt today.'

As it happened, much of the brunt was being borne in Scotland and the north-east of England, where Britain's intensive rearmaments programme was fast reaching a peak. 'However unfortunate and uneconomic to the country at large the cause of (this) revival may be,' Robert Bruce wrote cheerfully in 1940, 'it certainly had the effect of increasing the purchasing power of the worker in certain industries. The very nature of their toil – manual labour of the most arduous character undertaken in many cases under conditions of great heat – has always meant that beer was looked upon as a natural and necessary beverage. Consequently, there was a beneficial effect on the consumption of beer in the districts affected.'

The Blitz – fireboats tackle burning warehouses in London docks, 11 September 1940.

Even though more Younger's personnel served in the Second World War than in the First, their casualties were lighter.

Once again, in other words, pints were being lined up five deep on bars throughout Tyneside to quench the prodigious thirsts of coal miners, ship builders and munitions workers – and all in the name of the War Effort. Of course there was a down side. McEwan-Younger's overseas trade, Bruce admitted, had been far from satisfactory. 'Competition from foreign breweries is intense and the practice of establishing local breweries in the east and elsewhere is rapidly increasing . . . In India, a measure of restriction, if not prohibition, is steadily growing.' The trade with British troops abroad remained important, but transporting Scottish beer to war zones like north Africa was dangerous and expensive. Even in the UK freight was a heavy burden. A recent 5 per cent rise in railway charges looked like costing Younger's another £5,000 a year.

The company's London business was also, quite literally, receiving a battering. A landmine near Princes Wharf in October 1940, was followed by a high explosive bomb a month later and incendiary bombs in December. The following Spring, the premises were damaged by more bombs, another land mine, fire, anti-aircraft shells and blasts from nearby explosions. And many of Younger's London pubs were blitzed, including the company's two Blue Anchors, one in Chancery Lane, the other in Fenchurch Street, the Coach and Horses in Aldersgate, the Clachan in Mitre Court, the Carved Red Lion in Islington, the Golden Last in Cannon Street, the Mail Coach in Bishopsgate and the Sun-in-the-Sands in Blackheath. The London Commercial Restaurant and the Edinburgh Stores near the Law Courts were

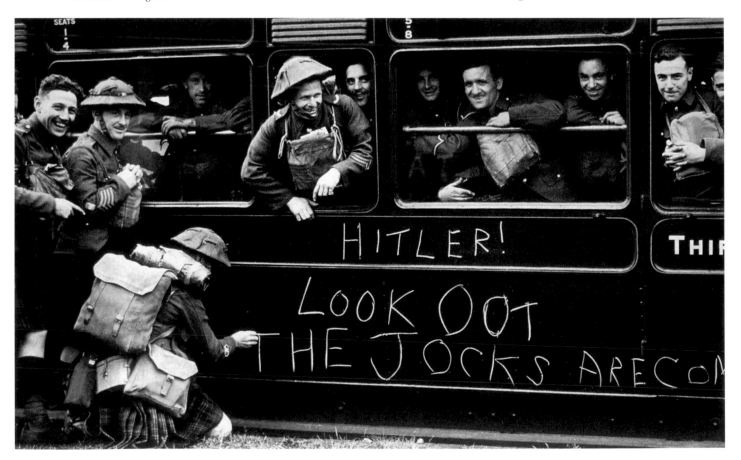

demolished by high explosives and flying bombs. Younger's store in Salford's railway goods yard, near Manchester, was bombed, and more than 600 casks, valued at £13,000 including their precious contents, were destroyed in its Belfast warehouse. Younger's pubs were also bombed in Sunderland, Hartlepool, Grimsby, Ramsgate, Middlesbrough, Bristol, Bridlington, Sheffield, Chingford, Coventry, South Shields, Stockton-on-Tees, Hull, Patrington, Chelmsford, Hastings and Dalmuir, near Glasgow. Four ships with Younger's cargoes were sunk, although only two were carrying full casks. And McEwan-Younger's bottling plant in Malta was so badly damaged by German bombing that it was given away after the war.

Younger's personnel escaped more lightly, even though 1,100 served with the armed forces or in civil defence, far more than in the Great War and a measure of the company's growth. But there were casualties. Harry J. Younger was killed near St Valery in Belgium in June 1940. But his cousin Charles survived severe fighting in Burma and William McEwan Younger, William Younger's second son, who had been made a director of McEwan's in 1935, also came home safely.

During the London Blitz bombs destroyed buildings surrounding this Younger's pub in Mayfair. Compare this photograph taken in 1946 with the recent one *overleaf.*

The Coach and Horses, Bruton Street, London W1. This surprisingly small pub, in the heart of Mayfair between Berkeley Square and New Bond Street, was constructed in the early 19th century. It was given its mock-Tudor façade in the mid-1930s. In the Blitz all the buildings adjacent to the pub were destroyed, leaving just the pub itself unscathed, *see previous page*.

10

Well Placed

Victory in Europe was greeted with national celebration, but the party was soon over. Waging war with Hitler's Germany had cost the UK dearly; the country had acquired debts of £3 billion and there were acute shortages of almost everything, including beer.

Back in Newcastle after a busy war, Edward Reed sought understanding for his company's plight in a series of advertisements headed *Post-War Problems*. One explained that the country's malting capacity had been seriously reduced by enemy action, malting labour was scarce, British hop supplies were limited and imports were barred. Even so, Newcastle Breweries was producing more beer than in 1939. But at a price. Another pleaded that the company had been forced to limit production by the Government and adhere to 'utility' standards. Its range of beers was curtailed and until controls were relaxed, it could not raise strength or restore choice. A third apologised for the state of the group's pubs. For six years, maintenance had been all but impossible, leaving Newcastle Breweries' houses and hotels shabby and run down. But while labour and materials remained closely controlled by the State, refurbishment was confined to essential work. Planning restraints were also frustrating plans to build new houses, even on 'greenfield' housing estates with no existing pubs near by. Although more moralistic influences may have been at work in these cases, Edward Reed's offer to provide portable pubs was turned down equally firmly.

Celebration in London,
on VE Day, 9 May 1945.

Clement Atlee, with his wife Violet, celebrating the Labour landslide in the 1945 General Election.

Centre: variations on the theme of Old Father William, from a Wm Younger's promotional tin tray.

Unveiling the memorial to the 23 employees of William Younger & Co. who lost their lives in the Second World War.

Newcastle Breweries' difficulties were shared by all brewers. In the first General Election after the war, the Labour Party had swept to power. Its mandate was to create a welfare state, with fair shares for all. But with so little to share, its only course of action was even more stringent rationing and controls. In 1946, brewers were instructed to curb production and reduce the strength of their beer. Tyneside's beer drinkers protested vigorously that they would effectively be paying the same price for more water. John Strachey, the Minister of Food, conceded that they had a point and promised to release more barley for beer manufacture as soon as possible. But in the immediate future all grain was needed for bread, itself heavily rationed, and animal feed for the coming winter. In the event, this was one of the harshest on record. In February 1947, coal supplies to 'non-essential' industries were slashed in half; many North Country brewers were forced to reduce production by the same percentage. The larger Scottish brewers were less affected, partly because they had been quicker to turn to electricity.

Scottish Brewers, indeed, was looking to the future with confidence. In spite of restrictions on beer output and strength, the group's profits in the year to 30 April 1946 had risen by 20 per cent after tax to £122,000. And this was an absurd understatement of its real performance. Younger's trading profit had totalled £780,000 and McEwan's had grossed £625,000. Only the combination of ever-higher duty and swingeing excess profits tax was keeping net earnings down to such modest levels.

The directors were not without their worries, however. Their breweries were in urgent need of redevelopment and Younger's pubs were as dilapidated as any. The group was also short of experienced management. William Bond, who had run the London office for nearly 30 years, had recently retired, as had Younger's long-serving head brewer, James Stevenson. Harry Younger was still chairman, but had spent the war in Devon and it was many years since he had taken an active role. Robert Bruce jnr remained a director, but he, too, was getting on. Archie Younger died a fortnight before Scottish Brewers' AGM in February 1947. Jock Younger, who replaced his uncle as deputy chairman, was a charming man who rode to the brewery each day on a bicycle. That left Charles Younger, who had joined the board in 1945.

The situation at McEwan's would have been as bad, but for the return of William ('Bill') McEwan Younger. Aged 40 at the end of the war, his slight build and horn-rimmed spectacles belied his distinguished war record; like Charles Younger, he had been awarded a DSO. He had another hidden advantage. When Margaret Greville died in 1942, she had left him all her equity holding in the business her stepfather had founded. Not only had the legacy given him unquestioned control of McEwan's, it had also made him the largest individual shareholder in Scottish Brewers. Harry Younger had been livid.

Diplomatically, Bill McEwan Younger concentrated on modernising the Fountain Brewery and restoring McEwan's trade. Increasing sales was difficult at first. Raw materials were still scarce and export quotas were hard to obtain, giving foreign competition even more time to consolidate its hold on McEwan-Younger's overseas markets. But the Labour Party's fragile command of the economy did not survive Stafford Cripps's devaluation of the pound in 1949 (in theory to deter imports; in practice the devaluation gave a kick-start to inflation) and in the early 1950s demand for Younger's Scotch Ale and McEwan's Export Ale boomed.

John Strachey, Minister of Food, second from the right, compelled by chronic post-war shortages to ration foodstuffs, instructed brewers to reduce the strength of their beer.

To begin with, the two companies were hard put to supply the market. But by the end of 1954, both the Fountain Brewery and Holyrood Brewery had been largely redeveloped. *The Brewers' Guardian* described the modernisation of the Fountain Brewery as one of the most complete in the industry, writing glowingly of the new boiler house, 'erected in such a manner that it can be extended on the south side if occasion

Newcastle United, FA Cup winners, 1951. Note the barrel, with the Newcastle Breweries star, indicating the long-term association between the club and the brewery.

should demand it in the future', and containing four Economic boilers, all with Green's Diamond Economisers, Clyde Soot Blowers and Davidson Grit Arrestors. 'Of particular interest are the coal-handling and ash-handling plants.' The brewhouse had been as extensively re-equipped, with Morton calorifiers fitted with automatic electric flow and temperature controls to heat the liquor instead of the old, coal-fired furnaces, and its seven coppers topped with pressure domes and given Worssam heaters, boiling fountains and coils. Worssam had also added false gunmetal bottoms to two mash tuns, in which the latest versions of Steel's patent mashing machines had been installed. 'Following the wort to the

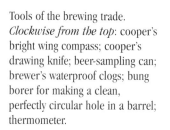

Tools of the brewing trade. *Clockwise from the top*: cooper's bright wing compass; cooper's drawing knife; beer-sampling can; brewer's waterproof clogs; bung borer for making a clean, perfectly circular hole in a barrel; thermometer.

Below: brewery workers, 1949. *Left*: bottling hall ladies at Queen's Park; *right*: Canonmills maltings.

fermenting block, one finds that this department also has been extended. In addition to adding eight new copper vessels, two new fermenting rooms have been constructed, each with sixteen copper vessels, all the new tuns having been constructed and installed by Archb. McMillan & Co, Edinburgh.' Alongside was a yeast installation 'of the well-known Scott's Yeast Plant type'. And in the Fountain's four acres of storehousing, casks were washed by new Super Goliath machines from Hopkins & Sons and moved about on a Lister 'Autotruck' with a specially designed 'tipper' at its rear.

McEwan's was also re-equipping its Glasgow depot and bottling plant, which was supplied with beer from Edinburgh in a dozen glass-lined, stainless-steel bulk tankers, six carried on railway wagons and six mounted on road trailers. And the company owned more than 25,000 11-gallon steel containers for its carbonated beer, of which two-thirds were used for exports and the rest went to UK army camps. A growing percentage of McEwan's exports of India Pale Ale and Red Label Sparkling Beer, however, was sold in cans made for the company by the Metal Box Co.

Rebuilding McEwan-Younger's export trade, though, proved far from easy. Hopes that devaluation of the pound would give British beer a price advantage were swiftly dashed as many of the UK's competitors followed suit. In any case, most of the group's overseas markets were in the sterling area. Instead, African sales were blighted by cloudiness in bottles of Red Label. Old stocks were bought in at a loss, but complaints continued to flood back. Efforts to revive trade with the oil companies in the Gulf were also thwarted by past experience of McEwan-Younger's sparkling beer, with more returns from the company's Baghdad agent. In the Far East, attempts to revive McEwan-

Younger's share of the Malayan stout market proved unsuccessful; sales to the Indian Army stumbled over prices; and more problems with Red Label affected business in Sydney. Only orders for the NAAFI and for on-board consumption on British ships remained buoyant, but even these stalwart markets were uncertain.

Reluctantly, Scottish Brewers began to accept that its export markets might never fully recover. And in 1955, the Abbey Brewery, which for some years had only been working part-time, mainly for McEwan-Younger, was closed down and turned into offices.

It was an unhappy period for Younger's. For the last seven years, it had been plagued by bad beer. Nothing the company's chemists tried seemed to make any difference to a persistent cloudiness, which severely damaged the appeal of Younger's ale, especially in the north-east of England, where consumers insisted on brilliance. The main suspicion fell on the quality or variety of the hops, although an alternative theory was contamination by an errant yeast which was somehow surviving the cleansing procedures. Gregor Eadie, McEwan's brewing director, had a simpler explanation. He blamed William Ferguson, who had been in charge of the Abbey and Holyrood breweries since the war ended.

Whatever the reason, the trouble steadily undermined Younger's competitiveness, especially with McEwan's. McEwan's trading profits passed Younger's in 1950 and in the year to 30 April 1954 reached £1m., nearly £200,000 more than Younger's gross earnings in the same period. After nearly a quarter of a century, the rivalry between the two businesses was still intense. But the balance of power was shifting in McEwan's favour, partly because its beers were proving more successful, but mainly because Bill McEwan Younger was beginning to stamp his authority on the whole group.

A turning point had been the death of Harry Younger in 1951. The amiable and unassuming Jock Younger took his father's place as chairman of Scottish Brewers and Bill McEwan Younger became deputy chairman. As such, he was effectively the group's chief executive, although he was careful not to let it show too clearly. But Younger's brewing problems proved a catalyst. In September 1954, William Ferguson resigned. He was replaced by William Harris from the Fountain Brewery, who arrived with strict instructions from Eadie to stick firmly to the basics. Within an embarrassingly short time, Younger's beers were as good as ever.

In itself, this did nothing to draw the two companies closer together. But wider influences were at work.

The underlying factor was a rise in property values. As Britain's economy began to recover, the value of High Street shops and offices, which during the war had collapsed, recovered. Shortages caused by war damage exacerbated demand, and rents and prices began to rise rapidly. Long before building restrictions were finally removed in 1954, entrepreneurs like Charles Clore and Maxwell Joseph had grasped the potential worth of property assets owned

The best long drink in the world—

Post-war example of the industry's 'Beer is Best' campaign.

Newcastle Breweries deliveries, early 1950s.

Edward Reed, who died at the age of 50, when he was about to take over as chairman of Newcastle Breweries in 1953.

Col. James Porter, with a formidable record in the brewing industry, was appointed chairman and chief executive.

by many long-established businesses. Brewers were prime targets, with their portfolios of public houses on prime sites and their large manufacturing premises, originally on the edge of town, but now often near the centre, owing to the spread of cities.

Breweries in the south of England were the first target. Several family businesses in London and the bigger provincial cities were snapped up by property developers and other, more expansionist brewers. An especially alarming predator arrived in the person of Edward Taylor, an aggressive Canadian who had made a vast fortune selling bootleg beer to prohibitionist America. Taylor bought the Hope & Anchor Brewery in Sheffield and used it as his base for a series of raids on other provincial companies. His technique was frighteningly direct. The first notice that most country brewers received of his interest in their businesses was a bid from Northern Breweries, as Taylor's UK holding company was initially named (it later became United Breweries), dropping on their boardroom tables.

Inevitably, the larger British brewers counter-attacked and Taylor's offers began to be contested. Courage, for example, beat him in a closely fought battle for Georges of Bristol. Smaller breweries also began to take defensive measures of their own. Some turned to 'white knights' like Whitbread, which acquired minority shareholdings in more than a score of regional companies. Others decided that attack was the best form of defence and launched their own campaigns.

Newcastle Breweries' first move was the acquisition of Robert Deuchar Ltd. Robert Deuchar was the third of four brothers who had moved to the northeast of England from Fife in the 1860s. He had turned his brewing business into a limited company in 1897 and two years later had bought a three-year-old brewery at Duddingston, near Edinburgh. In 1900, the company had taken over Simson & McPherson, which owned maltings in Edinburgh, a brewery in Melrose and a bottling plant in Newcastle, as well as a collection of public houses in and around Edinburgh, Glasgow, Newcastle and London. In 1952, the majority of the company's shares came on the market. A £1m. offer from Newcastle Breweries at the end of 1953 was accepted.

Celebration was muted. The group was still recovering from the shock of Edward Reed's death at the age of 50 earlier in the year. Alex McConnell, who had taken over the chair from Barras Reed, was on the verge of retirement and Edward had been about to take his place. Instead, James Porter became Newcastle Breweries' chairman and chief executive.

In his mid-sixties, Colonel Porter was the doyen of the brewing industry in the North-East. His father had been a master brewer in Burton-on-Trent and Porter had studied at the Birmingham School of Brewing before serving in the North Staffordshire regiment during the First World War, commanding its 6th battalion and winning a DSO and bar. Since joining Newcastle Breweries, he had dedicated himself to improving its beer. He still visited the brewery seven days a week and knew all its employees personally. But he was fully aware of the wider picture. Jim Porter had

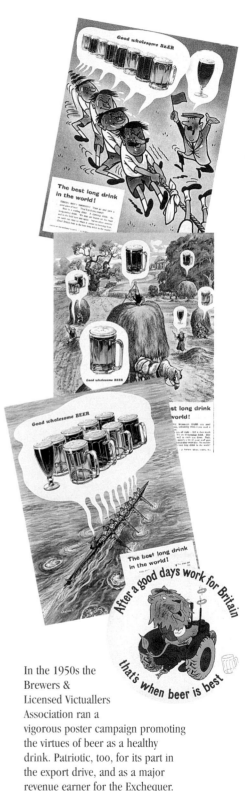

Newcastle Brown Ale bottles from the original to the Silver Jubilee, 1927–52.

become president of the Institute of Brewing as long ago as 1939 and he was deeply involved in the Brewers' Society, of which he was the current chairman. He lost no time in pressing forward with Newcastle Breweries' acquisition strategy by buying the business built up by the youngest of the Deuchar brothers, James.

James Deuchar had taken over the Allison brothers' Monkwearmouth brewery in 1888 and after the Great War he had acquired the Lochside brewery at Montrose to provide his public houses with an 'in-house' Scotch ale. He died in 1927, leaving his two breweries and 150 pubs to his children; Newcastle Breweries bought the lot in 1955, also for around £1m., although it recouped some of this investment by selling the Lochside brewery to Macnab Distillers two years later. The rest of Robert Deuchar's Scottish interests were also sold.

In 1955, too, the Northern Corporation was wound up, its portfolio of public houses and hotels bought back into Newcastle Breweries to remove the risk of a back-door raid on the group's property assets.

And at the beginning of 1959, the group took over John Rowell & Son of Gateshead. The Rowell business dated from 1846 and the company had since acquired a South Shields brewery, a wine and spirits firm, a mineral water manufacturer, a chain of public houses and a controlling interest in the Gateshead Brewery Corporation.

Scottish Brewers' expansion began in 1952 with the purchase by Younger's of a Newcastle firm of whisky distillers named John E. McPherson & Sons. In the same year, McEwan's took over the business left by Robert Deuchar's eldest brother, Alexander. McEwan's trade with Alexander Deuchar had survived his rough handling by William Younger in 1907, and the Edinburgh brewery had acquired 9,000 shares in his business in the 1930s and another 10,000 in 1946. The balance of Alexander Deuchar's equity was bought for just under £500,000 in 1953.

In the 1950s the Brewers & Licensed Victuallers Association ran a vigorous poster campaign promoting the virtues of beer as a healthy drink. Patriotic, too, for its part in the export drive, and as a major revenue earner for the Exchequer.

McEwan's advertisements of the 1940s and 1950s. The globe symbol, seen here on the can and bottles, would soon be replaced by the cavalier.

Bill McEwan Younger signalled greater ambitions in McEwan's annual report for 1954. 'The policy of retaining in the business a very substantial proportion of earnings,' he wrote, meant that the company was 'well placed to finance further expansion when suitable opportunities occurred.'

Before seeking these out, however, he determined that it was time to knit the two halves of Scottish Brewers into a single garment. Resistance from Younger's was half-hearted, following the debacle at its breweries, and in 1955 all the preference and debenture shares in both subsidiaries were exchanged for comparable stock in Scottish Brewers. The sum of the parts was formidable: the group's assets were conservatively valued at £12m. and cash reserves totalled more than £5m. (say £85m. in today's money). When Reid Brothers of Newcastle on Tyne, in which Younger's had held a minority interest for so many years, came on the market in 1956, buying out the other shareholders for £670,000 was small change.

In 1959, tax on beer was reduced by 2*d.* a pint, enough for publicans to reduce their on-the-counter price to 1*s.* a pint and stimulating 20 years of uninterrupted growth in UK beer sales. The reduction also helped inspire E. P. Taylor to raise the takeover stakes. Northern Breweries crossed over the border to seize in swift succession the Scottish brewing businesses of John Jeffrey and William Murray in Edinburgh, George Younger and James Calder in Alloa, John Fowler in Prestonpans and James Aitken in Falkirk. Obviously, there was no time to waste. In 1960, three of Edinburgh's remaining breweries, T. & J. Bernard, J. & J. Morison and Robert Younger, threw themselves into the arms of Scottish Brewers. But these, too, were small fry; the cash price for all three was little more than £2m., although there was an additional cost implicit in Bill McEwan Younger's promise that none of their employees would be made redundant. As a bulwark against a hostile bid from Northern Breweries, the three tiddlers were little use.

Potential Scottish partners of any size, however, were thin on the ground.

Only Tennent's of Glasgow had a capital of more than £2m. But when the Glasgow lager firm made an approach to Scottish Brewers, Bill McEwan Younger refused to pursue it on the grounds that it would create a virtual monopoly in Scotland. 'We must have competition,' he told his brother-in-law, Peter Balfour. 'Otherwise we'll all go to the wall.' In truth, he was also influenced by his belief that lager would never command a really large market. But he did not let his personal distaste for the thin, Continental-style beer stand in the way of Scottish Brewers acquiring the Red Tower Brewery in Manchester, which had just been rebuilt to make lager, and moving production of Younger's newly created MY Lager there.

Expansion outside Scotland, clearly, was a different matter. When James Porter asked if he was interested in a merger, Bill McEwan Younger was quick to respond. On 1 May 1960, Scottish Brewers combined with Newcastle Breweries to form a £50m. group named Scottish & Newcastle Breweries.

Jock Younger, chairman 1951–61.

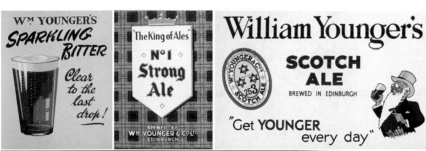

'King of Ales', a 1950s Younger's brand and examples of advertisements of the period.

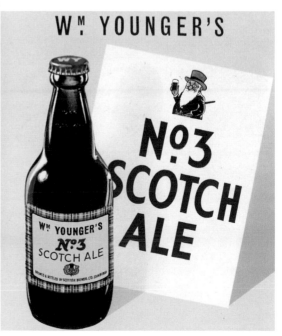

11

'The Pubs Were Awful'

It really was a merger. Shareholders in Newcastle Breweries received four million ordinary £1 shares for their business, equal to 35 per cent of the total equity of the new group. It was the first time that the owners of Scottish Brewers had issued shares to another company and Bill McEwan Younger hastened to stress that it would not happen again in a hurry. 'Size in itself has no particular merit and it is our view that a company such as ours, with a good growth record and, as we believe, in all normal circumstances a substantial further growth potential, should be very chary of diluting its ordinary capital . . . particularly at the high premiums currently being paid for companies in the drinks industry,' he said in his first statement as chairman of the new group.

But a glance at the balance sheet showed that Newcastle Breweries would have been far too expensive to buy for cash. Both groups had commissioned professional revaluations of their assets at the time of the merger: Scottish Brewers' portfolio of licensed premises, which had been valued five years previously, was raised by £4.5m. to £17m.; Newcastle Breweries' retail holdings, which had never been properly revalued, went up from under £4m. to £12m. Altogether, the combined assets of the new group were valued at £55m.; at a conservative estimate, buying Newcastle Breweries for cash would have cost Scottish Brewers £20m.

It was a good deal for the Tyneside brewery group as well, though. It had saved itself from the clutches of the dreaded Canadian and its operations remained under its existing management. And with James Porter as vice-chairman and joint managing director, Newcastle Breweries could be sure

Ye Old Leathern Bottle, Barkham, Wokingham, Berkshire, dates back to 1790. The original building was a Courage pub, and this was extended in 1993 to become a large pub-restaurant.

First meeting of the Scottish & Newcastle board, June 1960. Seventh from left: Jock Younger, president; on his left, centre, Sir William McEwan Younger, chairman; on his left, James Porter, vice-chairman; fourth from right, Charles Younger.

Fountain Brewery, Edinburgh, c.1910. These offices had remained largely unchanged until 1954 when Peter Balfour joined Wm McEwan, his first task being to mechanise the accounts.

that its interests were defended at the highest level. At least in the short term. Porter reached the age of 70 at the end of August 1961, and a special resolution had to be passed at the September AGM to allow him to remain a director. He was certainly needed, as Bill McEwan Younger was finding the task of reorganisation to be formidable.

Integrating recent cash acquisitions like T. & J. Bernard, J. & J. Morison and Robert Younger was no problem; they had really only been bought for their goodwill. Their breweries were closed and their customers offered a choice of Younger's and McEwan's beers. And the future of the Royal Moss Side Brewery in Manchester, as the Red Tower had been renamed, was neatly resolved by letting Guinness make its new Harp lager there, as part of a joint company for the manufacture and sale of Harp in the UK.

The main shareholders in Harp Lager were Guinness, Courage and Scottish & Newcastle (Bass initially held 5 per cent, but soon dropped out). To begin with, the new brand achieved remarkable success.

A marked increase in sales of bottled beer resulted from stocking McEwan's Export and Newcastle Brown Ale in all the 1,600 pubs owned by Scottish & Newcastle. On the other hand, the group was spending heavily on improvements and extensions at its three main breweries, especially Fountainbridge, and its maltings, bottling halls and licensed premises. These investments would undoubtedly lead to savings in production costs, but only in due course. In the meantime, Scottish Brewers and Newcastle Breweries continued to be run much as they always had.

Bill McEwan Younger was, however, beginning to put together a new management team. A key member was his 40-year-old brother-in-law, Peter Balfour, who had been tempted out of the Scots Guards into McEwan's in 1954. Balfour had found himself in a Dickensian office filled with clerks writing up huge ledgers with pen and ink. His first task had been to mechanise the accounts; his second had been to build up McEwan's vestigial chain of licensed houses. Within two years he was on the board of Scottish Brewers, almost literally Bill McEwan Younger's right-hand man, with a desk in the same office, from which he was ritually excluded when people like James Porter came to discuss confidential business.

New arrival Tim Lewis was another ex-serviceman, although one with eight years' experience of the wine and spirits trade prior to joining Scottish Brewers at Jock Younger's invitation in 1960. Lewis was put in charge of Mackinlay-McPherson, as the amalgamation of John E. McPherson and Charles Mackinlay was named. Newcastle-based McPhersons marketed a whisky named Cluny, which sold surprisingly well in California, plus a range of French, German and Spanish wines sold as La Tour Clerac, Prinz Rupprecht and La Chiqua. Other popular products included Windjammer rum, White Crystal gin and Timpano sherry. Mackinlay held an Edinburgh agency for French bordeaux and burgundies, as well selling its own brand of Scotch. But the real purpose of the subsidiary was to supply Scottish & Newcastle's pubs with wines and spirits.

Alick Rankin was given the job of developing Mackinlay-McPherson's presence in Scotland. Another new recruit, 25-year-old Rankin had joined Scottish Brewers in January 1960, after National Service in the Scots Guards and four years in a Canadian merchant bank. J. & J. Morison's old maltings in Edinburgh's Canongate were converted into a wine and spirits warehouse and depots were established in Aberdeen, Dundee and Inverness. A big store to serve the west of Scotland was also opened in Glasgow, backed up by another in Dumfries and a smaller one in Ayr. Each had a fleet of vans in Mackinlay-McPherson's green and gold-painted livery to make local deliveries. Similar depots were established south of the border in Kendal, Leeds, Manchester and London.

In 1962, Lewis brought in baronet Sir Hew Hamilton-Dalrymple as his assistant. Hamilton-Dalrymple was left in charge of Mackinlay-McPherson the following year when Lewis was made Scottish & Newcastle's group sales and marketing manager, while Rankin went to run Scottish Brewers' managed houses. By then Mackinlay-McPherson's US agent, Conrad Lewbel, had raised sales of Cluny so much that the Scotch whisky's sole wholesaler, Simon Levi of Los Angeles, could no longer supply the market. Scottish & Newcastle Importers Inc was formed in 1963 to break into other territories besides southern California, with Michael Dixon as its president and its head office in San Anselmo, 15 miles north of San Francisco's

Sir William McEwan Younger, first chairman of Scottish & Newcastle Breweries, 1960–70.

Brewing industry safety advertisement in the early 1960s.

Park Stores bottling plant, mid-1960s.

Golden Gates bridge. Exports of whisky to the USA, as well as imports of wines and spirits, were stored in bonded warehouses in Newcastle. Exports of beer went via London, but they were a shadow of their former greatness; Canada and Belgium were still buying reasonable quantities of strong Scotch ale, but competition from local brewers and the ever-increasing popularity of lager had undermined most overseas demand for Scottish beer.

Fortuitously, whisky was filling the void. Sales of Scotland's unique spirit were so great that supplies were in danger of running short. Scottish & Newcastle was already helping finance the redevelopment of a distillery on the Hebridean island of Jura, but it was obvious that more Scotch was needed. Jack Harris, Archie Jones's successor at Newcastle Breweries, and the designer of the Jura distillery, William Delmé-Evans, located a site in the heartland of the Scotch whisky industry, the Spey valley, which runs through the Grampian mountains in the Highlands of Scotland. It was a long-term investment. Glenallachie Distillery opened in 1968 with a capacity of 750,000 proof gallons a year, but it would be several years before the whisky was mature enough to drink.

Gavin Reed was another junior member of Scottish & Newcastle's management team. The same age as Rankin, Edward Reed's son had joined the family business five years after his father's death, having done his National Service, paid his own way through university and spent a year in a Manchester brewery. Following another year of general training in various departments, Colonel Porter invited him into his office to tell him: 'Gavin, I've come to the conclusion that hotels are different from pubs.' Newcastle Breweries owned eight hotels, of which only the Turk's Head and the County Hotel in Newcastle were of any size. The embryonic hotel division was the obvious recipient for four more hotels in the north of England belonging to Scottish Brewers following the merger in 1960. Reed was also given the challenge of building a first-class hotel on a 13-acre site at Gosforth Park Racecourse, three miles north of Newcastle.

In 1963, Reed was summoned to Edinburgh as group hotel manager. He quickly discovered that almost all the Scottish properties placed in his charge were 'commercial' hotels – a euphemism for Sunday boozers. Scotland's licensing laws allowed hotels to open on the Lord's Day to *bona-fide* travellers, so the country had lots of huge pubs with a statutory minimum of bedrooms – the number varied according to the licensing authority from four to a dozen or so. It was virtually impossible to run them as genuine hotels without changing them radically; something that nobody in Scottish & Newcastle wanted, as they were enormously profitable outlets for the group's beer.

A Younger's beer tanker c.1960.

Scottish & Newcastle helped finance the redevelopment of the Jura distillery as the group expanded its presence in the burgeoning market for whisky in the 1960s.

It was obvious, however, that the group's better-quality hotels needed a separate identity. Thistle Hotels was formed in 1965 as a management company for three existing hotels, the Angus Hotel, Dundee, the Royal Turk's Head, Newcastle, and the Golden Lion, Stirling, plus two under construction, the Gosforth Park, and the Strathspey at the Aviemore Centre in the Highlands, which was being developed as a major tourist centre – with the benefit of hindsight, the Strathspey's design proved to be as unhappy a choice as that of its architect – John Poulson.

Selling beer, however, remained far and away the most important part of Scottish & Newcastle's business. Tim Lewis's first challenge in his new job was making sure that the group's leading brands were on sale in all the pubs it supplied, of which the great majority were free houses. Newcastle

The Glenallachie Distillery was opened in 1968.

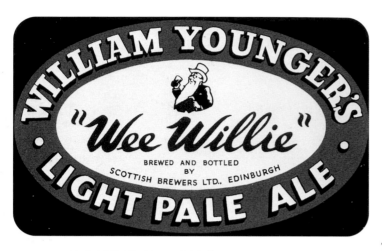

Early 1960s Wm Younger's label.

The introduction of the Breathalyser by Barbara Castle (right) in 1968 was a boon to sales representatives, providing a good reason not to drink with publicans.

Brown was popular with every landlord, as was McEwan's Export, but Younger's traditional Scottish beers were a harder sell in England, especially in the North-East where they were up against Newcastle Breweries' high-quality Exhibition Ale.

It was essential, however, for the morale of Younger's salesmen that at least one of Holyrood Brewery's labels acquired the same status as the leading brands from the Fountain and Tyne breweries. The choice was Younger's Special, which was a big seller in Scotland, but little known south of the border. One of the tactics chosen was to give it a distinctive Scottish identity by calling it Younger's Tartan Bitter. Another was to aim the beer at the young. The advertising campaign was so successful that Lewis found himself under attack from the Church of England for encouraging under-age drinking. Luckily none of the advertisements for Younger's Tartan Bitter pictured anyone under the age of 21. The group's newly combined sales force also pushed Tartan hard in working-men's clubs, which bought huge quantities of beer. Fortunately, the Scottishness of the product proved a selling point on its own.

Tim Lewis was the genius behind the campaign. Lewis was a brilliant leader, a charming, charismatic man who inspired the group's 300-strong UK sales force. He was a great showman, dreaming up a series of innovative marketing techniques such as the 'Tartan Club', a fleet of caravans which toured free pubs and clubs around the country offering a party night with free beer for their customers, with the landlord keeping all the profits. Ironically, the new brand's success created problems of identity in the beer's home market, with Scottish publicans gazing blankly at southern visitors asking them for a pint of Tartan. The answer was to relabel it in Scotland as Younger's Tartan Special. Within five years, annual sales of Younger's Tartan had risen from 100,000 to 1,000,000 barrels.

Not that Scottish & Newcastle's representatives had an easy life. The East End of London was an especially testing market, because many landlords took offence if salesmen refused a pint on the house and then expected the courtesy to be returned. Lewis found this out the hard way when he accompanied the group's local man on his rounds of Younger's houses. After two pubs and four pints, he had to stay in the car. The capacity of much of the sales force was awesome. But Lewis became very conscious of the toll that the job took. For all their convivial demeanour, many salesmen were often lonely. And their health was frequently undermined by alcohol. When Barbara Castle introduced the Breathalyser in 1967, it was a huge boon to the industry's representatives.

The job was no easier in Scotland and the north of England. Alick Rankin had been given a six-month taste of Glasgow's pubs in 1960, when he was put in charge of a group which averaged a murder a month. 'It was Glasgow at its very toughest and roughest and most horrible. People were demanding protection money everywhere and we had bouncers and protection guys. You grew up fast. If you went into a pub and you'd got a tie on, the place would go totally silent till you left. The pubs were awful – quite awful. None of them had windows – they were all bricked up.' Rankin was mugged twice and often frightened, but pride dictated that he did not try to disguise his management role. 'Anyway, if you sloped in trying to pretend you were someone else, they knew bloody well.' In his new job, Rankin set about raising standards in all the group's Scottish pubs, as well as buying more. He did the same in London and in Manchester, where the group had acquired a number of houses as part of the Red Tower brewery deal, which he discovered were every bit as tough as those in Glasgow.

A pub scene in the Gorbals area of Glasgow in the late 1950s.

Rankin had no authority over what happened in the north-east of England. Newcastle Breweries owned far more pubs than the rest of the group in that area and continued to run its own show as though the merger had never taken place. Nobody complained. Its pubs sold beer in quantities that most of Scottish Brewers' tenants could scarcely believe.

The growing demand was met by doubling the capacity of the Fountain Brewery and greatly expanding Scottish & Newcastle's output of bottled and canned beers – by the end of 1962, 40 per cent of the group's beer was in bottles or cans. To cope with the trend, Newcastle Breweries' huge bottling hall was modernised, a new hall was built in Northern Ireland, two extra high-speed bottling lines were added in Glasgow, and a brand-new bottling plant at Fountainbridge doubled capacity there. There were four canning lines in Edinburgh and two more in Glasgow. And new from Holyrood was an experimental 11-gallon aluminium keg to hold chilled, pasteurised, Tartan bitter.

Late 1960s Wm Younger's label.

More than half the group's beer was still traditional 'real ale', kept in wooden or steel casks which had to stand for a day or two before being tapped and needed constant attention. The final stage of brewing, in fact, was done by the publican. He kept the temperatures level and he vented the casks so that the yeast in the beer continued to ferment to exactly the right point. His skill was crucial. But rising wages and deteriorating labour relations made it increasingly difficult to ensure that these old-style beers were kept in good condition. The invention of the Barnes neck, a complicated device which let a liquid enter and exit a metal container through a single hole without contamination by air or dirt, made it possible to fill metal casks with a predictable, sparkling bitter which could be piped straight to the bar under pressure. At least, that was the theory. Jack

Harold and Mary Wilson celebrate Labour's election victory in 1964.

Harris struggled for a long time to overcome persistent corrosion where the Barnes necks fitted into the aluminium kegs. Sir William, as the chairman had become early in 1964, hailed the sensational success of the 'Clear-Flo' container, as Scottish & Newcastle named its metal keg. But the problems of corrosion were only finally solved when it became economic to use stainless steel. Nevertheless, more and more of Scottish & Newcastle's beer was sold in keg, in line with the rest of the industry. And, in spite of owning far fewer tied houses than its major UK rivals, who by the mid-1960s were down to five (Allied Breweries, Bass Charrington, Courage, Watneys and Whitbread), Scottish & Newcastle's sales continued to grow at a remarkable speed.

Admittedly, Scottish & Newcastle benefited disproportionately from building grants in Development Areas, which were extended to cover almost all of Scotland and the north-east of England. But Sir William was not appeased. 'One would have thought it inconceivable that any government would do other than encourage and stimulate an industry of great importance both to regional development and to our balance of payments,' he fulminated in his annual statement for the year to 30 April 1966. 'But, in fact, by excluding the industry from Investment Grants and imposing on it the full burden of Selective Employment Tax, the Government has done precisely the opposite; a situation the more fantastic at a time of an acute balance of payments crisis, with onerous measures recently imposed to meet it. The effect of this, of course, cannot be other than highly restrictive. So far as we are concerned, we have for some time been in process of reviewing drastically our quite ambitious plans, not only because of the cost of borrowing today, but of more importance because these substantial additional burdens will now often reduce the return on such capital invested, never high, to a quite unacceptable level.' It all, the chairman thought, added up to a sorry story. Record sales did nothing to ameliorate his pessimism.

Two years later he was a little happier. Pre-tax profits had climbed by nearly 10 per cent to a new record of £11m., owing to a marked increase in sales of keg beers throughout the UK; the performance of Keg Harp in Scotland was, in the chairman's mind, quite astonishing. But there was still plenty to complain about. 'To give but one example: the reference of the brewing industry to the Monopolies Commission has required our finance director (Halbert Renwick) to spend, in the last two years, the equivalent of fully three months of his time, dealing with the innumerable facts and figures required. In this and other similar references and investigations, all sense of priorities seems to have been lost. It will no doubt be argued that the tied house system has defects, but what is beyond question is, firstly, that largely as a result we have a very high and still rising standard of licensed premises of all kinds and, secondly, if defects do exist, they are wholly peripheral to the very grave economic and financial problems which confront the country today.'

He was equally unimpressed by new incentives to encourage the development of hotels by reducing SET, which he saw as likely to divert investment from development areas like the Highlands, and sharply critical of an industry-wide training levy imposed by the Hotel and Catering Industry Training Board. 'I entirely fail to see why a company with satisfactory training provision should be forced to subsidise others.'

Sir William was also unsympathetic to the Government's desperate efforts to control wages. 'It may be possible in an emergency,' Younger said dismissively, 'to impose a rigid system of controls of salaries and wages for a strictly limited period. But it is a crude weapon at best . . . When the Government itself, often in the face of strike action, acts in breach of its own laid-down policy, that policy can no longer be maintained without widespread and damaging industrial unrest.'

It was the pot calling the kettle black. The group had just backed down to strike threats from the Tyne Brewery's branch of the Transport & General Workers Union. Plans to save money by transferring long-distance deliveries from road to rail involved redundancies and loss of earnings for Tyne Brewery drivers. Scottish & Newcastle had only averted industrial action by promising to share the savings with the union's local branch.

And yet, reluctantly, Sir William had to admit that the group's prospects were good and a real possibility of growth existed. Scottish & Newcastle's future was firmly based on the popularity of such beers as Tartan Bitter, McEwan's Export and Newcastle Brown Ale. 'Most important of all, however, we have succeeded in building up a largely young and I believe very effective management team.'

The significance of this closing remark was made clear a year later, when Sir William McEwan Younger retired as chairman and chief executive at the age of 63.

SCOTTISH & NEWCASTLE
PUBS TODAY

The engraved glass mirrors are among many original features in the Old Toll Bar, Paisley Road, Glasgow. The pub is a listed building of special architectural and historical interest.

12

'Tell Them You're the Butler'

Sir William Younger's decision to retire was not a complete surprise. He had paved the way by appointing Peter Balfour as group managing director two years earlier. But few expected their chairman to cut himself off so completely from the business in which he had worked for 40 years. Captains of industry rarely turn their backs on everything that they have laboured to create. Bill McEwan Younger did not even want to become joint vice-president with Jim Porter, let alone usurp Jock Younger from the presidency. Nor was he tempted into an honorary role when both died two years later.

Sir William did not, however, leave a vacuum. He had meant what he said about a young and effective management team. Its leader was Peter Balfour, who became chairman as well as managing director, and new executive directors included Jack Harris, Gavin Reed, Newcastle Breweries' head brewer Michael Van Gruisen and its hugely effective sales director George Brown, James Porter's son Henry and John Archibald Younger's son David. Tim Lewis and Sir Hew Hamilton-Dalrymple were already on the board.

The old guard was still well represented, with Scottish Brewers' long-serving John Craster as deputy chairman and Michael Clutterbuck, a clever, multi-lingual member of the Younger family, made joint managing director. And Jim Porter kept a firm grip on the North-East. But there was a real feeling of new hands steering the corporate ship, which was, as Balfour had

Peter Balfour, chairman and chief executive from 1969 to 1983.

The Tattershall Castle, second vessel from the right, is a paddle steamer converted into a pub, on the Thames Embankment.

A new Harp Lager brewery in Edinburgh was opened by the Duke of Edinburgh.

Early 1970s Harp Lager label.

to confess, struggling to correct a slight wobble in its wake. In May 1969, a 'third-generation' computer had been installed to invoice customers. Its programming was inadequate and it broke down. By the autumn, Scottish & Newcastle's billing system was weeks in arrears. Fortunately, many customers continued to settle their accounts without being billed. At the end of the financial year to 30 April 1970, delays in cash collection were down to two weeks, but that still added up to a £4m. shortfall. Balfour spoke bitter words about 'this extremely expensive piece of equipment' and the 'much additional cost in the form of consultants' fees and other expenditure' that it had incurred.

In spite of this, the group had ample funds to finance its expansion plans, which included boosting production in Scottish & Newcastle's Edinburgh breweries by 50 per cent over the next five years by building a new brewery at Fountainbridge. The Duke of Edinburgh had also just opened a new Harp lager brewery in Edinburgh, built next to the Holyrood Brewery and capable of producing 350,000 barrels a year. Scotland's appetite for lager continued to confound the sceptics.

For the first few years of the 1970s, the UK economy boomed under the relaxed rule of Edward Heath's Chancellor of the Exchequer, Anthony Barber. Demand for Scottish & Newcastle's beers blossomed as never before. It seemed as though the only problem was one of supply. Some customers waited up to six months for kegs of Tartan. In the West Country, Courage in Bristol, Wadworth in Devizes and St Austell's Brewery in Cornwall distributed the group's beers, but elsewhere Scottish & Newcastle had to invest heavily in additional distribution facilities. After nearly 40 years, the group's London organisation abandoned the *faux* Tudor charms of Princes Wharf for a steel-framed brick box in Acton. And new depots were opened in Manchester, Birmingham, Luton, Southampton and Bristol to meet rampant demand throughout the county.

Unfortunately, the popularity of Tartan turned out to be less than robust. Compared to English bitters, it was on the sweet side; the post-war baby-boomers to whom Lewis had appealed so successfully liked this to begin with, but as their palates matured, they switched back to more traditional southern bitters. The big swallowers in the Midlands were never keen; Scottish & Newcastle's salesmen made huge efforts to get its kegs into the large working-men's clubs in and around Birmingham, only to see them thrown out again after a month or so.

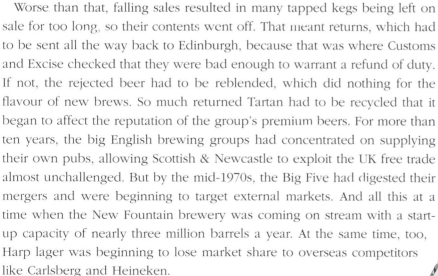

Left: 'Tartan' bus, Trafalgar Square, London, during a 1972 sales campaign.

'We're behind you Scotland', Younger's support for the national team in the 1978 World Cup.

Worse than that, falling sales resulted in many tapped kegs being left on sale for too long, so their contents went off. That meant returns, which had to be sent all the way back to Edinburgh, because that was where Customs and Excise checked that they were bad enough to warrant a refund of duty. If not, the rejected beer had to be reblended, which did nothing for the flavour of new brews. So much returned Tartan had to be recycled that it began to affect the reputation of the group's premium beers. For more than ten years, the big English brewing groups had concentrated on supplying their own pubs, allowing Scottish & Newcastle to exploit the UK free trade almost unchallenged. But by the mid-1970s, the Big Five had digested their mergers and were beginning to target external markets. And all this at a time when the New Fountain brewery was coming on stream with a start-up capacity of nearly three million barrels a year. At the same time, too, Harp lager was beginning to lose market share to overseas competitors like Carlsberg and Heineken.

Even so, sales kept on rising. The development of North Sea oil and gas had brought unexpected prosperity to Scotland and the north-east of England. And Scottish pubs also benefited from a relaxation of their country's licensing laws following the Clayson

Committee's report in 1974. Ten years before similar changes in England, Scotland's pubs were allowed to extend their opening hours, open on Sundays, and admit children. The reforms had a dramatic effect and in time led to the transformation of the industry throughout the UK. Scottish & Newcastle, which had led the lobby for change, was granted Scotland's first all-day and family licences.

Other areas of the group continued to do well. Scottish & Newcastle bought 27 pubs in Cumbria when the Carlisle State Management Scheme was closed down in 1973. Thistle Hotels had grown under Gavin Reed's management into a substantial business, with 36 three- and four-star hotels, mostly in Scotland and the north of England. The hotel division expanded very rapidly in the late 1960s and early 1970s under the stimulus of government grants and incentives which the largely Scottish board was unable to resist exploiting to the full. Gavin Reed fought hard to raise the quality of fittings and furnishings, but bowed to pressure for as many bedrooms as possible by skimping on their size. For example, he saved £54,000 by cutting 18 inches off the diameter of the 170-bedroom Strathallan Hotel in Birmingham, which was built in the round on a very small site in 1973. He would happily have put the space back again once he had experienced what the new hotel's rooms were like to sleep in. But that did not stop it making money. Although not during that year, which was a bad one for the hotel industry.

The wines and spirits division was expanded in 1973 by the acquisition of Christopher & Co., a long-established London wine merchants. Canongate Wines was formed to sell Christopher's wines, along with those imported by Mackinlay-McPherson, throughout the UK. All the group's wine and spirits activities were merged under the title Waverley Vintners, which was put under the charge of Alick Rankin, who was made a main board director. Rankin then went off to the USA with Peter Balfour, where Michael Dixon persuaded them to buy the Simi Winery in northern California on the basis that it presented a splendid opportunity to get into the fast-growing US wine market, albeit at a cost over the first three years estimated at £350,000. Other diversifications within the group included a joint venture into oil-rig catering, a golf and leisure centre at St Cyprien in southern France, and an agreement with Del Monte Corporation to manufacture frozen foods at a new factory in Lanarkshire.

In volume terms, 1974 was a good year, with sales of beer and lager totalling more than four million barrels for the first time in the group's history. A trading agreement with Cadbury Schweppes, which put Scottish & Newcastle's canned beers into supermarkets throughout the UK, accounted for a large part of the improvement. Net profits, however, were 25 per cent down on the previous year's record of £14m. And even this decline concealed the straits which the group had experienced during the year. On several occasions, Balfour had faced the prospect of paying Scottish & Newcastle's wage bill out of bank borrowings.

The main reason for the cash crises was an alarming deterioration in margins, owing to a 23 per cent rise in the cost of cans, more expensive fuel as a result of the OPEC crisis at the end of 1973 and the coal-miners' confrontation with Heath (although the three-day week in January 1974 did little harm to publicans' takings), and a 100 per cent increase in the price of barley. The introduction of VAT was no help, either. Nor was a £600,000 buy-out of the agreement to share savings from delivering beer by rail instead of road with the Tyne Brewery branch of the TGWU.

When Newcastle Breweries struck this deal in 1968, it had failed to establish that it was for one year only. An industrial tribunal ruling that the agreement carried no time limit left the management at the mercy of the union. The big increase in beer brewed and packaged at the Tyne Brewery over the next five years led to large payments to the members of the branch, whose demands became ever more exorbitant. One provocative request had been funding for a competing, union-owned brewery. Another had been for Scottish & Newcastle to buy the champion racehorse Arkle for the branch! Peter Balfour admitted to shareholders that the settlement was a very large sum, but told them it was certainly in the long-term interests of the company.

It did not, however, resolve Scottish & Newcastle's poor industrial relations, which stretched back for a long time. The group was not alone. Unions had seized the initiative throughout British industry and the authority of many managers was becoming seriously eroded. Peter Balfour did his best to improve the situation and took Allan Blacklaws, the group personnel director, on a tour of European companies to study work councils and other ways of co-operating with labour.

In 1975 inflation rose to 25 per cent as Harold Wilson's re-elected Government strove vainly to bring the economy under control. With the state controlling prices and unions holding employers to ransom, the effect

The discovery of oil under the North Sea brought unexpected prosperity to Scotland and north-east England.

Facing page: All the group's wine and spirits businesses were merged, under the name of Waverley Vintners, in 1973.

Scottish & Newcastle's canned beers went on sale in supermarkets throughout the UK.

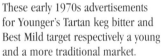

These early 1970s advertisements for Younger's Tartan keg bitter and Best Mild target respectively a young and a more traditional market.

The popularity of keg beer led to bulk distribution in tankers such as this one photographed in 1972.

on the group's financial position was dire. Since 1971, the capital employed by Scottish & Newcastle in its business had all but doubled to £225m. But net profits of £10.3m. in 1975 were 6 per cent less than they had been five years earlier. In real terms, shareholders' earnings had halved over the period.

It was a low point. The next year saw a fall in the rate of inflation and a recovery in sales of beer. Harp lager moved to counter competition by introducing Kronenbourg and Scottish & Newcastle began to test market its own brand, McEwan's lager, in north-east Scotland. Thistle Hotels moved back into profit after a couple of bad years and Waverley Vintners increased its trading profits. The Simi winery, though, was sold at a loss of £1m. The US wine market had turned down and the fall in the value of the pound made the cost of servicing the dollar loans raised in New York to buy the winery far too expensive. Alick Rankin took the setback philosophically.

Golf St Cyprien, however, was going full-steam ahead and Scottish & Newcastle had bought out its partner in the £6m. leisure project, which included a 27-hole golf course and an estate of holiday villas. It was another mistake. When the golf club opened, its membership was pitifully small. The French, it transpired, were nothing like as keen to join an expensive golf club in the Languedoc-Roussillon as its promoters had hoped. Nor were they queueing to commission large, luxurious villas around the golf course.

Faced with a £600,000 loss in 1976, the first full year of operation, Golf St Cyprien hastened down market with plans to let bedrooms in the club house and build large numbers of small holiday homes on part of its land. To no avail. The venture lost another £600,000 in 1977 and prospects of Golf St Cyprien ever making money receded into the distance. The scheme was sold to the owners of a French ski resort for a nominal sum and Scottish & Newcastle wrote off its entire investment. 'Would it not have been wiser, Mr Chairman,' a shareholder asked Balfour sarcastically at the next AGM, 'to have bought a golf course in California and a vineyard in the south of France?'

Del Monte Kitchens, too, proved to be a loss-maker and was sold to Ross Foods. Scottish & Newcastle also shed its investment in the Aviemore winter sports centre to House of Fraser, although it kept the Strathspey Hotel. The group's attempts to diversify, it had to be confessed, had not been fruitful. The losses were not serious in the context of Scottish & Newcastle's overall activities, but they contributed to a minor crisis of leadership. Peter Balfour had decided it was time to retire as chief executive, but found it hard to name a successor. It had recently become apparent that Michael Clutterbuck was suffering from Alzheimer's disease. Jack Harris, Tim Lewis and Halbert Renwick were all at or near the group's retirement age of 60. In any case none of them were candidates. Forty-three-year-old Gavin Reed, who had tried desperately to make the project work, was still shaken by the Golf St Cyprien misadventure. And Alick Rankin? Well, Peter Balfour had never found Alick the easiest person to get on with; he had an annoying tendency to speak his mind.

The alternative was an outside appointment. Balfour's choice was 49-year-old Robert King, a senior executive at Metal Box, who joined Scottish & Newcastle in October 1977.

His arrival was followed by a shuffling of top jobs. Gavin Reed was put in charge of Waverley Vintners as well as Thistle Hotels, and Alick Rankin was made marketing director of Scottish & Newcastle's beer company, with Michael Van Gruisen responsible for production. Christopher Chalmers was recruited as finance director. And Bernard Kilkenny was brought in as managing director of the beer company.

The same age as King, Kilkenny was a much respected figure in the brewing industry. A quiet, thoughtful man, he had been managing director of Allied Breweries, at the time the second largest beer producer in the UK. But he had fallen out with Allied's chairman, Derek Holden Brown. Persuading him to join Scottish & Newcastle had been a coup. Kilkenny was an expert brewer, he had integrated beer businesses, he knew how to move beer production from one brewery to another, he understood marketing and distribution, and, perhaps most important of all, he had plenty of experience of dealing with intransigent unions.

Scottish & Newcastle's industrial relations on Tyneside were still appalling. A stoppage in November 1977 had resulted in a serious loss of

Label celebrating Newcastle Brown Ale's Golden Jubilee, 1927–77.

Younger's labels.

Sandy Bell's bar in Edinburgh, 1973.

The 'winter of discontent',
1978–79: Newcastle City workers
voting to strike.

business to other suppliers and Allan Blacklaws' consultative processes were making slow progress. Kilkenny told the board that the only answer was to undermine union power by fragmenting the group's distribution system. The giant warehouses and transport depots in Edinburgh, Newcastle and London were replaced by eight satellites outside the three cities. The strategy worked, although its benefits took time to show through.

A more conciliatory approach to the unions was pursued in the Chairman's Forum, a unique gathering created by Balfour and Blacklaws in response to the Bullock Report on industrial democracy. The forum met twice a year and embraced representatives of every bargaining group in Scottish & Newcastle, both unions and management, as well as all the executive directors. Around 60 people were involved. At the meetings, the board explained the progress of the business and its strategy for the future, including such thorny subjects as rationalisation. Strictly confidential information was shared with junior management and union bosses. Any questions could be asked and the only taboo subjects were personal grievances or specific issues, such as on-going pay negotiations. The forum was also a vehicle for education about wealth creation in general and how this influenced Scottish & Newcastle's business and profits. More progress, though, was probably made at lunch, when directors and senior managers sat next to shop stewards and staff representatives.

But evidence that the management was winning hearts and mind was slow to emerge. In 1979, Balfour tried a more direct approach in the form of a report to employees on the group's performance. Under the headline 'We've been standing still too long, now's the time to MOVE AHEAD', charts showed that after allowing for inflation, Scottish & Newcastle's sales had all but stood still since 1973 and profits before tax had fallen by 40 per cent. Even more worrying was a substantial fall in the volume of beer sold from the peak in 1975. Perhaps Peter Balfour hoped that Margaret Thatcher's victory over James Callaghan's beleaguered Labour Government that May had inspired a change of heart in the unions. He was to be disappointed. Converting entrenched attitudes was a gradual process. It was several years before Scottish & Newcastle could claim to have overcome its industrial relations difficulties.

Changes were, however, taking place. One was in the group's lager interests. At the end of September 1979, Harp lager was put into liquidation and its assets shared between its partners. In exchange for its 32 per cent shareholding and £5m. in cash, Scottish & Newcastle acquired the Royal Moss Side Brewery in Manchester and the Harp Brewery at Holyrood, plus a franchise to brew and sell Harp brands through all its pubs and off-licences. The investment in Harp Lager had been very rewarding, but with the lager market continuing to grow, all three partners had begun to believe they might do better on their own. The break-up left Scottish & Newcastle with two modern breweries in which to make its own brands of lager as well as Harp; indeed, it would have to work hard to sell all that Manchester could produce, although transitional arrangements would ease this problem until 1982.

At the same time, Waverley Vintners took over Gough Brothers, which owned 200 off-licences in the south-east of England.

And a tourist boom in London gave Gavin Reed the opportunity to expand Thistle Hotels in the south of England. Reed had already persuaded the board to buy the Kensington Palace Hotel from the reclusive Barclay twins in 1977. The price had been £3.75m., which worked out at less than

The Conservatives were returned to power in May 1979. Margaret and Denis Thatcher arriving at 10 Downing Street.

Cannizaro House Hotel, Wimbledon, was the first of Thistle's Country House Hotels.

Labels for export to North America, with a strong emphasis on the Scottish connection. Note the use of Younger's Father William to promote McEwan's beer.

McEwan's crown cork beer bottle tops use the Cavalier logo and conventional spelling of the company name, unlike the North American labels.

£12,000 for each of the hotel's 320 bedrooms, well below the current cost of building. Two more London hotels, the Lowndes and the Cadogan, were bought from the Barclays a year later. Now Reed was determined to make Thistle Hotels a significant presence in the hotel industry. He did not have long to wait. In 1980, Peter Balfour was telephoned by Reo Stakis. Stakis had come to Glasgow after World War II to sell lace made in Cyprus. Balfour had supported him with a loan from Scottish Brewers when he decided that the drinks industry offered greater potential. By the end of the 1970s, Stakis had acquired a large number of public houses and become one of Scottish & Newcastle's most valued customers. Now he was calling to give Balfour the inside information that EMI was planning to sell its loss-making hotel and restaurant division. Balfour, Gavin Reed and Chris Chalmers flew to the south of France to meet with Lord Delfont, EMI's chairman, who was at the Cannes annual film festival. They arrived at Delfont's luxurious apartment as he was leaving for a preview. 'Wait for me,' he instructed. 'What shall I say if anyone calls?' Balfour asked. 'Tell them you're the butler.'

Delfont's price was £23m. After selling off the Angus Steakhouse chain for £3m. and setting previous losses against tax, the net cost of EMI's hotel group to Scottish & Newcastle was £16m.

Any illusions that life was going to be easier under a Tory Government, however, were soon dashed. The fall of the Shah in 1979 plunged the industrial world into recession. In the UK, prices soared and jobs vanished. The result was inevitable. In 1981, beer consumption fell for the first time for two decades. At the same time Margaret Thatcher's Government was locked in fierce conflict with the trades union movement. Legislation to reduce the power of organised labour provoked further disruption in the public sector, culminating in the miners' strike in 1984. Scottish & Newcastle was quicker to improve its own industrial relations. A bitter five-week strike in the North-East over a new bonus system effectively ended the power of 8/223 Branch of the TGWU, which had remained a thorn in the company's side ever since the bonus system buy-out in 1974. A national three-year deal covering pay and conditions was agreed in 1982. This was reinforced by a savings-related share option scheme and, two years later, a profit-sharing scheme which for the first time gave employees a personal interest in the company's performance.

Beer sales, however, were still on the decline. The best Peter Balfour could hope for was a slow return to past volumes. Bad weather added to

the woes of publicans. Sales of whisky held up, but margins were under severe pressure. Only Thistle Hotels was flourishing. A glance at Scottish & Newcastle's record showed only too clearly that its performance was still far from convincing. Although turnover in 1982 at £620m. was up by 40 per cent compared to 1978, profits attributable to shareholders were down from £22m. to £18m. over the period. Allowing for inflation, earnings per share had halved yet again in real terms.

All that Peter Balfour was able to offer shareholders in his annual statement that summer was the hope that the weather stayed fine. There were far too many uncertainties on the domestic and international scene to make any promises. As well as chairman, he was once more group managing director. Robert King had failed to make a lasting mark on Scottish & Newcastle and had left the previous September. Balfour was privately prepared to take some of the blame for this. Perhaps he had interfered too much. Whatever the reason, his return as chief executive could only be temporary. At 62, he was already past the retirement age for executive directors. But who was going to take his place?

SCOTTISH & NEWCASTLE
PUBS TODAY

The Ravensworth Arms, Lamsley, Gateshead. The mother of Catherine Cookson was a chambermaid here, and her father popularly believed to be a gentleman visiting the near-by Ravensworth Castle. Lewis Carroll is reputed to have written *Alice in Wonderland* here for one of his daughters, and all the rooms are now named after characters in the story.

13

Envious Attention

Alick Rankin was not the first choice to succeed Peter Balfour as group managing director. But at the end of the day he was the best. He was backed by Scottish & Newcastle's deputy chairman, David Nickson, who had been chief executive of the publishers William Collins. Nickson had long realised that Scottish & Newcastle's poor profit record made it vulnerable to a takeover. What the group badly needed was a strategy which would restore its reputation as an aggressive, successful market leader. That required a dominant chief executive to make it happen. Of the various candidates for the job, it was obvious that Rankin came closest to this description.

Peter Balfour handed over his executive powers on 1 May 1983, after another difficult year. British arms had wrested the Falklands back from the Argentine the previous summer, but the UK economy was still in turmoil, in spite of or because of the Tories' monetarist policies, and the outcome of the General Election the coming June appeared far from certain. But the Falklands factor undermined the Left and Margaret Thatcher's majority quadrupled. The heart went out of organised labour, although unofficial strikes continued to disrupt Scottish & Newcastle's business. One on Tyneside in October 1983 was in support of a worker fired for urinating into a barrel of cider. It lasted a week. 'What did the strike achieve?' Scottish & Newcastle's new managing director asked rhetorically on the front page of the *Tartan Star*, the group's employee newspaper. 'Nothing whatsoever.' And Rankin warned that the board would not turn its back on tough decisions. To prove the point, he cut the personnel department from 128 to 22.

SCOTTISH & NEWCASTLE
PUBS TODAY

The Llandoger Trow, Bristol. The name comes from a sailing barge which used to ply between Bristol and the village of Llandoger in South Wales, 'trow' being the type of craft. It was one of the last half-timbered buildings erected in Bristol, before the style went out of fashion in the 1660s after the Great Fire of London.

The relative strength of the take-home market helped sales of canned beer.

Industrial relations, however, were already much better. The number of man-days lost through stoppages during 1983 was only 552, compared to 2,342 in 1982 and 7,828 in 1981. Over the same period, nearly 5,000 jobs had been shed, bringing Scottish & Newcastle's workforce down to 22,000, a fall of 20 per cent from the peak of 28,000 in 1980. Along with the drop in numbers had come an increase in productivity and a reduction in costs. In spite of the poor trading conditions, internal savings had pushed pre-tax profits up by nearly 30 per cent.

Fundamental to this improvement was the decision made a couple of years earlier to sacrifice sales volume rather than margins. Beer consumption was still falling and there was little hope of this being reversed. Instead, Scottish & Newcastle had decided to concentrate on quality. One example of this was a return to cask-conditioned beer.

The Campaign for Real Ale had led the backlash against the gassy blandness of keg bitter and the brewing industry was being forced to defer to customer demand for a return to more traditional treatment of beer. Scottish & Newcastle's response was McEwan's Best Scotch and Younger's Scotch Bitter, which were supplied in 11-gallon aluminium casks shaped more like wooden barrels than the group's standard, straight-sided 22- and 36-gallon kegs. Other nods to real ale were wooden bungs and final 'dosings' of each cask with yeast and finings. Their drawback was that the beer went stale quite quickly, which explained the smaller casks, and the cask-conditioned ales were not really expected to be big sellers. A much greater contribution to group earnings came from a new premium lager named Kestrel, which was proving hugely popular.

Most of the marketing effort concentrated on Kestrel and other premium brands, such as Beck's, a German lager for which the group had recently obtained a UK distribution agreement, and of course McEwan's Export, Younger's Tartan and Newcastle Brown Ale. The relative strength of the take-home market helped sales of canned beer, which had expanded enormously since the agreement with Cadbury Schweppes. Scottish & Newcastle Breweries (Sales) was launched in May 1984, to develop sales to home consumers on a national basis. Led by Alistair Mowatt, who had taken Alick Rankin's place as marketing director, the new company was an instant success.

Meanwhile, Bernard Kilkenny and Roy Summers, who had succeeded Michael Van Gruisen as production director, pursued a merciless campaign of modernisation and ratio-nalisation. Nostalgia might be a good sales

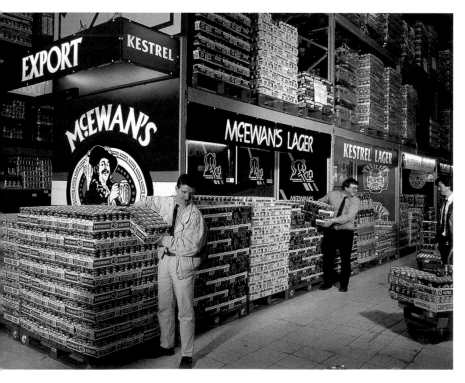

technique, but it could not be allowed to stand in the way of profits. In January 1985, the last Scotch ale was brewed at Holyrood as part of an overall plan to transfer all production in Edinburgh to the New Fountain Brewery.

An equally severe approach was taken in the rest of the group. Thistle Hotels was thriving under the management of Ian Hannah, a professional hotelier from EMI who had been picked by Gavin Reed to run all the group's hotels. But Waverley Vintners was having a much rougher ride. A study of the highly competitive wines and spirits market in the Home Counties resulted in three-quarters of Gough Brothers' off-licences being sold to Seagram for a profit of £3m. over the cost of acquiring the entire chain four years earlier. And after several years of contending with overcapacity and competition in the whisky industry, Scottish & Newcastle disposed of its Scotch whisky interests to Invergordon Distillers.

Control room in the
New Fountain Brewery.

This pragmatic approach made it another good year for earnings. In July 1985, David Nickson, who had become chairman of Scottish & Newcastle following Peter Balfour's retirement in October 1983, reported that profits had more than doubled over the past three years. Admittedly, some of this was due to the revival in the UK economy, but most of the credit could be taken by Alick Rankin and his compact executive team.

Cost saving and rationalisation was only one part of Rankin's strategy. Scottish & Newcastle remained vulnerable to a takeover as long as the City saw its management as defensive and reactive. With the active support of David Nickson, Rankin was determined to change this opinion.

His first move was a deal with the Barclay brothers to buy a Hartlepool brewing company from Ellerman Holdings in exchange for £35m. in cash and nine Thistle hotels. J. W. Cameron owned 460 public houses, most of them in Yorkshire and Cleveland. In spite of assurances that Cameron's brewery would not shut, the bid was referred to the Monopolies and Mergers Commission on the grounds that it would create an undesirable concentration of public house ownership in the North-East, which caused it to lapse. Rankin was extremely put out, describing opposition to the takeover as prejudiced and politically minded.

Newcastle United's Alan Shearer.
Scottish & Newcastle continue to
sponsor football clubs.

The negotiations did, however, serve to establish a working relationship with Morgan Grenfell, which had been hired as Scottish & Newcastle's merchant bank in place of Schroders. Links with the group's City advisers were further strengthened by the success of an agreed bid for Moray Firth Maltings, which was bought for £23m. in January 1985.

The following March Rankin raised his sights with a £110m. offer for Matthew Brown, a similarly sized brewing company to Cameron but based

Alick Rankin was appointed group managing director in 1983, becoming chairman in 1989 until his retirement in 1997.

in the north-west of England, where Scottish & Newcastle only owned 83 pubs. Once again the offer was referred, but this time the MMC concluded that a merger was not likely to operate against the public interest, even though Matthew Brown had recently acquired Theakston's, a small but high-profile brewery in north Yorkshire. Scottish & Newcastle renewed its bid, which to its disappointment failed, leaving it with just under 30 per cent of Matthew Brown's equity. Rankin stated doggedly that he would be making another attempt to buy Matthew Brown as soon as the Stock Exchange's rules on takeovers allowed.

Rankin next tried to buy Courage. Ironically, the two brewing companies had come close to merging twice before, once in 1968, when Sir William McEwan Younger had been chairman, and again in 1974. On both occasions the stumbling blocks had been personal; the first time over who would be chairman, and the second time the realisation by Courage's directors that, as Scottish & Newcastle would be the larger partner, the head office would be in Edinburgh. Since then Courage had fallen into the hands of Imperial Tobacco, which in turn had been swallowed by Hanson Trust. Serious discussions took place, but James Hanson made it clear he wanted a quick sale, with no risk of a reference to the MMC. When John Elliott of the Australian group Elders arrived with a cash offer of £1,500m., Lord Hanson accepted at once.

An agreed takeover of the Home Brewery, which owned a modern brewery and nearly 500 pubs and licensed premises in and around Nottingham, for £120m. was a consolation. The acquisition was completed in September 1986. A year later Scottish & Newcastle renewed its attack on Matthew Brown with a new offer valuing the company at £190m. This time the terms proved irresistible. Matthew Brown's Workington Brewery was closed and Theakston's was fenced off as an 'independent' operation selling

A section of the mural at the Fountain Brewery, installed in the 1980s.

traditional beer to the Free Trade. Theakston's Best Bitter, XB and Old Peculier were objects of veneration among real-ale fanciers. Gavin Reed told Newcastle Breweries' production department to leave the old-style brewery in Masham alone, instructed his salesmen not to discount its beers, however much they cost, and turned Theakston's master brewer and cooper into national characters comparable to Father William. Paul Theakston was not amused and resigned to set up the Black Sheep Brewery next door.

The integration of Matthew Brown and Home Brewery lifted Scottish & Newcastle's share of the UK beer market above 10 per cent for the first time, as well as giving it 2,300 public houses spread throughout Scotland, the north of England and the east Midlands, plus a small but valuable tied estate in London and the Home Counties. In spite of a still static market, the beer company's profits in the year to 30 April 1988 were up by 20 per cent to more than £100m. Admittedly, this included earnings from wines and spirits. Christopher & Co. had been sold in July 1987, leaving Waverley Vintners a shadow of its former self, and with Home Brewery and Matthew Brown running their own wines and spirits wholesaling operations, the logic of a separate division to manage Scottish & Newcastle's wines and spirits sales to its own pubs had disappeared.

Thistle Hotels, in contrast, was going from strength to strength, with operating profits 30 per cent higher. New hotels were being bought and built, and the company had won a Queen's Award for Exports in spite of a sharp rise in the value of sterling against the dollar. In his statement in July 1988, Sir David Nickson, as the chairman had become, reported contentedly that since Alick Rankin's team had taken over five years earlier, profits before tax had increased by an average of 22 per cent per annum, with earnings per share rising at an annual rate of 17 per cent, both well above inflation and the average performance of most British companies. Shareholders' dividends for the year totalled £20m. and £4m. was allocated to the 10,000 employees who qualified for the group's profit-sharing scheme.

There was only one piece of sad news, which was the death of Chris Chalmers at the age of 50. The new finance director was Brian Stewart.

The group's growth, Alick Rankin declared in his review of operations, had taken place at a time when competition in its two main trading sectors had never been more intense. It had been an active year, he reported, with capital expenditure on hotels, licensed premises, and plant and equipment totalling £87m. Flexible opening hours for public houses had at last been legalised in England, ten years after Scotland, and Scottish & Newcastle was continually

Malt production at Moray Firth.

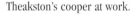

Theakston's cooper at work.

upgrading its pubs to make them more attractive, with a strong emphasis on better eating out in the North of England, under the Chandlers and Manor House brand names. The group was not trying to encourage more drinking but to respond to a change in consumer demand. 'It is only right to point out that producers of alcoholic beverages in Britain today are in the forefront of the attack on alcohol abuse,' Rankin added. He was beginning to appear rather magisterial. He had been appointed deputy chairman in succession to Sir Hew and he was vice-chairman of the Brewers' Society, as well as a member of the CBI's Scottish Council and a director of the Bank of Scotland. But that did not make his comments any less relevant. The brewing industry was more sensitive than ever to criticism and Rankin was among the leaders of its defence against the anti-alcohol lobby. 'Alcohol is too often labelled as the cause rather than the manifestation of wider social problems,' Rankin argued. 'Per capita consumption in the UK puts us 24th out of 27 countries with similarly structured and developed lifestyles. Only a small percentage of some 38 million consumers are guilty of alcohol abuse or are the victims of the disease of alcoholism.'

He exuded confidence in the future of Scottish & Newcastle. The UK was booming under the financial guidance of Nigel Lawson. At least, the South of England was booming. In Scotland and the North, unemployment remained over 13 per cent, although there were pockets of affluence. North Sea oil was still providing over 100,000 jobs and Scotland's 'Silicon Glen' employed more than 40,000 (mostly women) producing 15 per cent of European output of integrated circuits. Edinburgh was also becoming a major provider of financial services, with a sizeable population of affluent young professionals patronising its restaurants and wine bars. 'Post-industrial' development in other northern cities such as Glasgow and Newcastle, though, was only a veneer over much urban deprivation.

Alick Rankin, however, spoke of the combination of Britain's political stability and strong economy, which made the country 'the focus of envious attention from foreign interests'. Prophetic words. On Monday, 17 October 1988, Elders IXL announced a bid for Scottish & Newcastle which valued the group at £1.6 billion.

The board rejected it out of hand. Sir David Nickson went on television to say that it would not be in the interests of share-holders or employees for Scottish & Newcastle to be taken over by an Australian group, and later the same day a token force from the Fountain Brewery waved placards warning him to keep his hands off their company at John Elliott when he arrived in Edinburgh. A day later, when the Lord Mayor of Newcastle

Scottish & Newcastle employees and supporters marching through Edinburgh to protest at Elder's takeover bid in November 1988.

pressed a button to start the Tyne Brewery's latest high-speed bottling line, the bottles of Newcastle Brown Ale emerged with their labels upside down in protest against an Australian takeover.

Early in November, 5,000 Scottish & Newcastle employees, led by the captain of Rangers Football Club and other personalities, marched along Princes Street in protest against the bid by Elders. Alastair Darling, MP for central Edinburgh, and Alick Rankin addressed the rally. Four days later, 600 employees caught a special train from Edinburgh, nicknamed the 'Pommie Granite Express', to lobby 10 Downing Street. As the train arrived in Newcastle to pick up more protesters, the news came through that the bid was being referred to the Monopolies Commission. The announcement was not officially relayed to Elders, which took advantage of the lapse to increase its stake in Scottish & Newcastle by 10 per cent to 23 per cent. All that Lord Young, the President of the Board of Trade, could promise in redress for this breach of the takeover code was that the extra shares would have no voting rights.

The Commission took more than four months to arrive at its decision. But on 21 March 1989, it ruled that the merger would reduce consumer choice and competition between brands. Elders would be certain to introduce Fosters lager into Scottish & Newcastle pubs at the expense of other lagers. The takeover would restrict competition in Scotland and in the supply of beer to off licences and free houses. And by bringing together Scottish & Newcastle and Courage, which Elders had already acquired, the merger would result in two groups (the other was Bass) controlling more than 40 per cent of Britain's beer supplies. The MMC could find no benefits to offset these dangers and also noted the concerns expressed about the effects of Scotland's largest industrial employer losing its independence.

The victory was acclaimed by everyone from Malcolm Rifkind, the Tory Secretary of State for Scotland, to Campbell Christie, general secretary of the Scottish TUC. And a sigh of relief was expelled by all Scottish & Newcastle's employees, who had found it only too easy to believe that the takeover would have cost many of them their jobs. Most of the group's shareholders, too, expressed their pleasure, even though the MMC's ruling deprived them of a short-term profit; indeed, Lord Young's instruction to Elders to reduce its holding to 9.9 per cent over the next 12 months meant that Scottish & Newcastle's share price was likely to weaken unless something was done to stimulate it.

The group's market rating was also threatened by the MMC's report on the supply of beer, ironically published on the same day

Sir David Nickson, chairman 1983–89.

Scottish & Newcastle's in-house newspapers celebrating the failure of Elders' bid.

The Flying Scotsman, sponsored
by McEwans in the 1980s.

as its ruling against Elders. This showed that the six major brewers produced three-quarters of the beer sold in the UK and owned three-quarters of all tied pubs. It also revealed that the price of a pint had risen by 15 per cent in real terms between 1979 and 1987, almost double the rise in restaurant prices, lager sold for 10p a pint more than bitter, in spite of a very small difference in production costs, and pub prices varied by up to 20p a pint between regions, while beer in supermarkets cost the same throughout the country. The result, the MMC claimed, was a monopoly operating against the public interest. And it recommended a ceiling of 2,000 on the number of pubs owned by any brewer, freedom for tied houses to buy 'guest' draught beers and other drinks from alternative suppliers, and a ban on future loans to so-called free houses which effectively tied them to the brewery which lent them the money.

What the report was going to say had been worrying the brewing industry throughout the two and a half years it had taken to compile. Its conclusions were everything they had feared and Lord Young's announcement that he was 'minded' to implement its recommendations in full was a body blow. Even Scottish & Newcastle, the smallest of the Big Six, would have to sell off 300 pubs. As indeed it decided to do immediately, rather than wait for 1992, when the new Beer Orders were scheduled to come into force.

In most other respects, in fact, the changes looked likely to benefit the group. Already the leading supplier to the free trade, Scottish &

Newcastle was an obvious provider of 'guest' beers' to tied houses. And Alick Rankin had never been enthusiastic about making loans to publicans; they were, he thought, a very inefficient way of using capital. On the other hand, it could not be denied that the overall impact of the Beer Orders on the industry would almost certainly be adverse.

It was in these circumstances that the board decided to sell Thistle Hotels. This had done extraordinarily well throughout the 1980s, with pre-tax profits in 1989 up to £25m., and its prospects seemed better than ever. It is always hard to sell on a rising market, but it is always right. The sale was completed in November 1989, at the 'very satisfactory' price of £645m., which gave the group a capital profit of more than £400m. By then, the decision about what to do with the money had already been made: investment by Scottish & Newcastle in far less formal areas of the leisure industry.

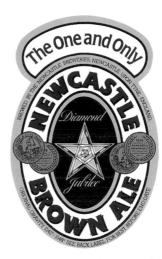

Newcastle Brown Ale's Diamond Jubilee label.

Fountain Brewery with Edinburgh Festival fireworks in the background.

Brewhouse, Berkshire Brewery, Reading. The brewery is
the largest in the United Kingdom, second in Europe.

14

Britain's Biggest Brewer

In July 1989, Scottish & Newcastle put Thistle Hotels on the market. It was a huge shock to many shareholders and employees who saw the hotel division as the jewel in the group's crown. Gavin Reed, who had founded Thistle and been responsible for so much of its growth, was naturally saddened by the decision, although he accepted the logic behind it.

Scottish & Newcastle stated that the reason for seeking a buyer for Thistle was to achieve 'a significantly higher return to shareholders by reinvesting the money elsewhere'. The general assumption was that the decision was motivated by the need to placate institutional shareholders, who had been looking forward to recording a fat profit on their investment following the Elders takeover. In fact, the possibility had been aired before John Elliott made his bid. Although Ian Hannah had raised the profitability of Thistle's management to an impressive level, he could do little about the fact that the business was capital-intensive. It was also obvious that the market for good hotels, especially in the south-east of England, was at a peak. Following the successful defence against Elders, Brian Stewart argued persuasively that the right strategy was to sell Thistle and move into other less developed areas of the leisure industry. Pontin's, for example.

As it happened, Scottish & Newcastle already had an option over 16.5 per cent of Pontin's equity as a result of helping its chairman, Trevor Hemmings, buy the company from Bass in 1986.

Scottish & Newcastle's relations with Hemmings went back several years, to when it had bought seven public houses that he had built in Lancashire from one of his private companies. Hemmings was a business phenomenon. He had started his first construction business in his teens with a capital of £12 and sold it at the age of 35 in 1970 for £1.5m. By then he had already built one holiday village for Fred Pontin, and between 1971 and 1972 he was responsible for the development of another, at Prestatyn in north Wales. Hemmings acquired a large shareholding in Pontin's in 1975 and joined the board the following year as Sir Fred's heir apparent; a restructuring was followed by the sale of Pontin's to the Leisure and General group, which in due course resold it to Bass. Five years later Hemmings resigned from Bass and in 1987 bought Pontin's back. Scottish & Newcastle's share option was one reward for helping Hemmings put together the buyout; another was 50 per cent of Pontin's purchases of beer for its holiday camps.

Pontin's played a key role in Scottish & Newcastle's successful expansion into the leisure and sports market.

In the course of renewing his business connection with Scottish & Newcastle, Trevor Hemmings made a presentation to the group's executive directors on the future of the leisure industry in Europe. Alick Rankin never forgot it; in his enthusiasm, Hemmings scorched the boardroom table with the teapot. Rankin's lips tightened but he did not let the incident blight their relationship. Within a short time, Hemmings had agreed to let Scottish & Newcastle buy 50 per cent of Pontin's, with an option on the remaining equity.

Included in Hemmings's presentation to Rankin and his close colleagues was a promotional film about a sporting goods superstore in Amsterdam called Sports Haus Centrum. Founded by Piet Derksen in 1953, this had swiftly grown into a chain of 17 branches. In 1978, Derksen sold Sports Haus Centrum to concentrate on an even more profitable venture which he had begun in 1967 with the purchase of a tract of unspoilt forest in the south-east of Holland, near its border with Germany. On this land Derksen built a small complex of holiday villas, equipped with luxuries like central heating and colour TV, and supported by modern sports and leisure facilities. A long way up-market from Pontin's, the complex was an immediate success and by the beginning of 1989 had grown to twelve villages known as Center Parcs, of which eight were in Holland,

two in Belgium, and one each in France and the UK (Sherwood Forest). Each Center Parc had as its centrepiece a huge, transparent dome housing a semi-tropical environment filled with swimming pools and exotic plants. Outside the domes a large choice of sporting and leisure activities was available to the occupants of, in total, nearly 8,000 holiday villas and apartments. By then Derksen was over 70 and looking for a suitable buyer. At least ten companies expressed interest; Hemmings made sure that Scottish & Newcastle was one of them.

Piet Derksen already knew Trevor Hemmings and saw him as someone with the drive and vision to develop Center Parcs across Europe. Even so the negotiations took several months, but eventually Scottish & Newcastle reached an agreement to buy 65 per cent of Center Parcs NV for £210m. At the same time, the board agreed to take over the remaining 50 per cent of Pontin's in a cash and shares deal. And it decided to finance the two purchases by selling Thistle Hotels.

Finding a buyer for Thistle Hotels did not take long. The company had done extraordinarily well throughout the 1980s, with pre-tax profits in 1989 up to £25m., and its prospects seemed better than ever. S. G. Warburg organised a classic City auction and at the end of September 1989, Scottish & Newcastle accepted a 'very satisfactory' offer of £645m. from Mount Charlotte Investments which gave the group a capital profit of more than £400m.

Center Parcs joined the group shortly after the acquisition of Pontin's. Its holiday villages in France, Holland, Belgium and the UK made Scottish & Newcastle a major player in the leisure market.

It was a turning point in Scottish & Newcastle's history. Alick Rankin became chairman as well as chief executive, with Gavin Reed as group managing director. Trevor Hemmings was appointed to the board with responsibility for Pontin's and Center Parcs.

In the next two years, to everyone's gratification, all the group's strategies paid off handsomely. Center Parcs and Pontin's did extremely well and beer sales rose, outperforming the industry by a remarkable 5 per cent. In spite of double-figure inflation, crippling interest rates, collapsing consumer confidence and widespread bankruptcies as Margaret Thatcher's long-running economic boom imploded into recession, Scottish & Newcastle's profits rose and rose again, reaching £216m. before tax for the year to the end of April 1991. Rankin decided the time had come to hand over his executive powers and chose Brian Stewart as the new group chief executive. Ian Hannah headed up a new division to manage all the group's pubs and other retail outlets. And Gavin Reed was made chairman of the beer company, which was named Scottish & Newcastle Breweries Ltd when Alick Rankin announced that the group was to drop the word 'Breweries' from its registered plc name 'in order to express better our wider horizons'.

The Government had adopted many of the Monopolies and Mergers Commission's 1989 recommendations, giving brewers who owned more than 2,000 licensed premises until 31 October 1992 to sell or to release from tie half the number above this total. On the surface, Scottish & Newcastle was undamaged by the new Beer Orders. Bringing its own pub ownership below the ceiling had been an excuse to dispose of the less profitable. And the Order requiring the Big Five to allow all their tied premises to sell a cask-conditioned draft beer made by someone else after 1 May 1990 had been one of the reasons why Scottish & Newcastle's beer sales had risen during the subsequent two years.

But that did not mean the group was free of risk. 'Our industry remains in a state of enforced change; a state which will continue for some years to come as manufacturing capacity contracts and multiple licensed retailers form new groupings,' Rankin warned shareholders in July 1992.

The next 12 months saw little improvement in the economy, although the devaluation of sterling in September 1992, following its ignominious withdrawal from the European Exchange Rate Mechanism on 'Black Wednesday' by Chancellor Norman Lamont, did begin to lessen the pressure. On the other hand, demand for beer continued to fall and Scottish & Newcastle's beer division struggled to maintain sales and profits. Highlights were a 30 per cent growth in sales of Theakston's and improvements by Beck's, McEwan's Export and Newcastle Brown Ale.

The performance of Center Parcs, in contrast, was better than expected and Scottish & Newcastle was quick to buy the outstanding 35 per cent of the equity. Ian Hannah's retail division, though, was feeling the strain of self-improvement, although its margins remained higher than for beer. Poor pubs were being weeded out, many more were being refurbished, a staff

training centre had been opened in Newcastle to upgrade standards, new marketing concepts, such as 'T. & J. Bernard' traditional ale houses and 'Homespreads' family food outlets, were being introduced, and the group's brands were being merchandised more professionally. Hannah had also divided Scottish & Newcastle's licensed estate into four companies: Scottish Inns, with over 400 pubs in Scotland; Tyne Inns in the north-east of England, with 479 pubs; Pennine Inns, with 525 pubs in the north-west and Yorkshire; and Trent Inns with 437 pubs, most of them around Nottingham.

The new names were a symptom of a fundamental shift in management strategy. For the first time, Scottish & Newcastle's retail outlets were being treated as profit centres in their own right, and not merely as conduits through which to sell beer. Ian Hannah applied the same approach to running pubs that had underpinned his success as a hotelier. Standards were set that transformed the division from a motley collection of individual small businesses into an integrated organisation with a unified management philosophy and consistent levels of service and presentation. It was an impressive achievement. There was only one problem. Scottish & Newcastle still owned far too few pubs in the southern half of England and Wales to make full use of its new retail skills.

Milnes of Rose Street, Edinburgh, won the 1993 national Pub Design of the Year award after being redeveloped as a T. & J. Bernard traditional ale house.

Above and below: the Chef & Brewer chain was acquired in 1993.

Brian Stewart was acutely aware that Scottish & Newcastle needed a high-quality national retail network if it was to compete with the likes of Bass and Whitbread. And he realised that the Beer Orders gave him a once-only opportunity to create one. His target was Grand Metropolitan's Chef & Brewer estate.

Grand Met (now part of Diageo) had been founded by Maxwell Joseph after the Second World War as a property company. In 1972, Joseph had astounded the City by taking over Watney Mann for the then impressive price of £200m. It was a David and Goliath deal which stretched Grand Met's resources throughout the 1970s, but eventually Joseph and his deputy, Stanley Grinstead, worked through their financial difficulties and began to exploit Watney's treasure chest of undervalued assets. In 1982, Joseph died and over the next decade Grand Metropolitan became the UK's tenth largest company, excluding privatised State monopolies like British Telecom. Its operating companies included Berni Inns, International Distillers & Vintners, Mecca Bookmakers, Express Foods, Alpo Petfoods, Inter-Continental Hotels, Pearle Vision and many others, as well as Watney Mann and Chef & Brewer. Its brand names in beers, wines and spirits were legion.

The Beer Orders made Grand Met rethink its strategy. With around 5,000 tied houses, it was one of the principal targets of the MMC report. Grand Met decided that its best strategy was to make radical changes to its relations with its publicans and stop brewing beer entirely. In 1991 it reached an agreement with Courage and its parent company, Fosters Brewing Group of Australia, as Elders IXL had been renamed. The first half of the deal gave Courage ownership of all Grand Met's breweries. The second lumped 7,350 pubs, including all of Courage's licensed estate and three-quarters of Grand Met's, into a jointly owned company named Inntrepreneur Estates Limited. Every landlord joining Inntrepreneur Estates had to accept a new 20-year lease which some welcomed for the opportunities it offered (a number became millionaires) and others disliked for the responsibilities it included.

But that still left Grand Met the owner of the Chef & Brewer estate, which owned more than 1,600 pubs, the majority of them in London and the south-east of England. Only 560 of the Chef & Brewer's pubs had become members of IEL. The rest were kept separate, a few because their landlords refused to join IEL or they were unsuitable in other ways, but most, more than 900, because they were large managed houses on prime sites where Grand Met owned the freeholds or leaseholds with more than 50 years to

Main picture: yeast room, Berkshire Brewery.
Inset: the brewery is a familiar sight to motorists on the M4.

On 18 May 1995, Scottish & Newcastle acquired Courage.

S&N reaches brewery deal with Courage

By Martin Waller

Courage deal makes S&N UK leader

THE SCOTSMAN
SCOTLAND'S NATIONAL NEWSPAPER

Corporate Scotland takes courage

S&N take Courage

S&N prepares to take Courage

Scottish & Newcastle's and Courage's beer brands have been combined under the name Scottish Courage.

Van loads of beer crossing the Channel for illegal resale has become an increasing problem for the British brewing industry.

run. Their capital value was obvious. Sir Alan Sheppard, Grinstead's successor as Grand Met's chairman, decided the quickest way to unlock it was to put Chef & Brewer on the market.

Stewart approached the acquisition of Chef & Brewer with extreme caution. He was nervous of alerting potential competitors, in particular Bass and Whitbread, both of which he feared would do their best to block any serious incursion onto their territory. It was also the first takeover campaign that he had conducted personally, instead of working through Warburg and other advisers. Scottish & Newcastle managers and surveyors surreptitiously spied out every Chef & Brewer pub. Thanks to tight security, none of them was detected, although their covert surveillance spread over several months. Their reports revealed that many of Chef & Brewer's houses had been starved of investment and badly needed refurbishment. Brian Stewart calculated that, as it stood, the Chef & Brewer estate was worth a little over £500m. He was reluctant to pay more, but the strategic value of the company to Scottish & Newcastle was patently much greater.

The price, however, was only one aspect of the complicated deal. Keeping all the Chef & Brewer pubs would have increased Scottish & Newcastle's total pub ownership to around 3,300, far above the ceiling set by the Beer Orders. To avoid this, Stewart agreed to sell more than 450 Chef & Brewer houses to Morgan Grenfell, which guaranteed to find another buyer for them as soon as possible. He also pledged to dispose of nearly 300 of Scottish & Newcastle's own houses within six months. Then there was the question of Courage's exclusive contract to supply Chef & Brewer's pubs with beer until March 1995. Finding the money to pay for Chef & Brewer was another challenge, requiring a two-tier rights issue of 100m. new shares. Doggedly, Brian Stewart and his team worked their way over or around every hurdle. After a great deal of hard bargaining, some of it with his own colleagues, Stewart offered Grand Met a price of £622m. No counter-bids arrived and Sir Alan Sheppard finally accepted in September 1993 at a meeting in his office in Henrietta Place, London. In celebration, the chairman of Grand Met poured glasses of pink champagne and sent out for Burger Kings. Stewart raised his glass enthusiastically. He knew he had pulled off an incredible coup. 'In one bound', as Sir Alick Rankin reported to shareholders, Scottish & Newcastle had achieved the scale and scope to compete in the premier league.

The job of integrating Chef & Brewer into Scottish & Newcastle Retail fell into Ian Hannah's capable hands. It was a formidable task, involving substantial disposals and redundancies, and without the retail skills that Hannah had introduced would have been far more difficult. The Beer Orders meant that all the group's tenancy agreements had to be renegotiated, and considerable investment was required in many Chef & Brewer pubs. The value of the acquisition, however, was soon obvious, with the retail division's operating profits in the year to 30 April 1995 rising by 60 per cent to £142m., compared to £88m., itself a new record, achieved by Center Parcs and Pontin's, and £82m. earned by the beer division, a drop of £4m.

The beer company did not have to suffer the ignominy of third place for long. In May, Sir Alick Rankin announced that Scottish & Newcastle was to acquire Courage for £425m. It was scarcely a surprise. There was no denying the fact that the Beer Orders had intensified competition, although the picture was blurred by the flood of cheap drink from the Continent. From 1 January 1993, as part of the European Single Market, British visitors to France could buy beer taxed at only 4.2p a pint; in the UK, the duty was over 30p a pint, more than seven times as much. The only limit on the quantity brought back was an assurance by the purchaser, if asked, that it was for personal consumption. Within two years, imports had risen by 150 per cent to over one million pints a day.

Throughout 1994, the Brewers and Licensed Retailers Association monitored the inflow. The number of van loads of beer crossing from Calais to Dover each day ranged from a low of 150 in March to a high of 570 in December. Much of this was patently for illegal resale. A survey of 300 pubs throughout England revealed that a third of their customers had been offered bootlegged beer in the year. No wonder Sir Alick argued in his chairman's statement for 1995 that members of the Single Market must accept common tax and tariff policies. Instead, he said scathingly, Kenneth Clarke, who had succeeded Lamont as Chancellor of the Exchequer, had just slapped a further duty increase on alcohol 'simply because he

Royal Brewery, Manchester.

Canning process at the
Royal Brewery.

Brian Stewart, chief executive.

Beamish brewery in Ireland, one of six breweries that Courage brought to the group.

couldn't think of any other quick way to solve his budgetary shortfall. Political insensitivity linked to fiscal illogicality, unpackaged and unadorned.'

Perhaps more significant, though, was the growth in demand for legally imported premium lagers from the Continent and elsewhere. Whatever the reason, Britain's 60 surviving brewery companies were under enormous pressure. Speculation about a marriage between Scottish & Newcastle and Courage had been rife for some time before it was formally unveiled.

It created a formidable alliance. Courage owned six breweries, including John Smith's of Tadcaster, Webster's of Halifax and Beamish & Crawford in Cork in the Republic of Ireland, its own two in Bristol and Reading, and Watney's brewery on the Thames at Mortlake, which was let to Stag Brewing to make Budweiser. Combined with Scottish & Newcastle's breweries, they accounted for a quarter of the UK's production of beer. Scottish Courage, as the combined beer company was to be called, would be Britain's biggest brewer, with annual beer sales in excess of £2 billion. It was an extraordinary development.

The acquisition also brought the group a portfolio of powerful brands, including John Smith's and Webster's Yorkshire Bitters, Courage Best, Directors, Beamish Stout, and Foster's, Holsten Pils and Kronenbourg 1664 lagers. Press speculation during the negotiations had made much of the potential conflict between brand owners such as Beck's and Holsten or Miller and Coors. Patient negotiation and the company's hard-earned reputation as an open, honest and reliable partner brought every single brand into the new portfolio. A valuable part of the deal was a partnership to brew and distribute Foster's brands across Europe. Scottish & Newcastle obtained the Foster Brewing Group's 50 per cent shareholdings in the UK companies marketing Holsten, and a production arrangement for Budweiser.

Courage's chairman, Mike Foster, hailed the creation of Scottish Courage as 'the perfect fit'. The combined company, he said, would have the resources to become a significant force in Europe. 'The purpose of this transaction,' he claimed, 'is to grow the enlarged business, not to shrink either Courage or S&N. The geographical fit and the brand fit are what add real value to the merger of the two businesses.' And Brian Stewart added that the skills and experience of Courage's 4,800 employees were two of the most highly prized elements of the deal.

Bar 38, Covent Garden, London.

The cheers from Courage's workers were muted. They would believe their jobs were safe when the savings of £40m a year from merging operating resources and reducing overheads, which Stewart was promising shareholders in Scottish & Newcastle, who were paying for the takeover by subscribing to another rights issue, had been made. And what would happen when Courage's contract to supply Inntrepreneur Estates ran out in 1998? They were right to be sceptical. Within two years, the combined workforce of Scottish Courage fell from 8,700 to 6,600. The only consolation was that the pain was shared. Webster's Brewery was closed, with the manufacture of Webster's Yorkshire Bitter transferred to John Smith's Brewery at Tadcaster. But so was Scottish & Newcastle's Home Brewery. Cuts to the combined distribution network were equally even-handed.

The successful integration of the two businesses was a remarkable achievement by Guy Dickson and a Scottish Courage Board drawn from both companies. Two recent large-scale UK brewing mergers had been characterised by sharp falls in market share, customer loyalty and employee morale, as well as failures to meet their financial targets. The importance to Scottish & Newcastle of quickly absorbing Courage into the group without losing its trade customers was clear.

All employees were told that plans for the reorganisation would be announced within six months. In the event, the review was completed in five. Scottish Courage retained almost all its customers, increased its market share, and delivered the financial benefits of the merger ahead of schedule.

As many of the job losses as possible were by natural wastage, although

Sir Alistair Grant, chairman since 1997.

Brian Stewart, presents Sir Alick
Rankin with a specially
commissioned silver cockerel
(the Courage symbol) on his
retirement in January 1997.

this was not, perhaps, how Sir Alick Rankin regarded his retirement in January 1997, at the age of 62. He left in the comforting knowledge that Scottish & Newcastle would soon be reporting record turnover and profits. Indeed, looking back over his 37 years with the company, its growth had been quite astonishing. His place as chairman was filled by Sir Alistair Grant, formerly chairman of Safeway, who had been a non-executive director of Scottish & Newcastle since 1994.

The price being paid by less fortunate ex-employees was referred to by Sir Alistair in his first chairman's statement in July 1997. He also acknowledged the increasing pressure on surviving employees to cope with new technology and growing demands for higher levels of customer service. And he warned, 'Management of our cost base to enable us to succeed in an increasingly competitive market place remains a key issue.' In other words, further job losses were possible. But he refrained from adding, as he could easily have done, that Scottish & Newcastle's remaining 45,000 workers had reason to count their blessings. Compared to most of the UK brewing industry, the group was an island of prosperity. Its share of British beer production had risen to nearly a third and Scottish & Newcastle had just bought another 310 pubs from the Grand Pub Company, as Inntrepreneur Estates had been renamed by its new owner, Nomura.

There was no question about the group's commitment to its licensed estate. During the financial year to 30 April 1998, it spent £120m. on improvements to its retail outlets, which ranged from ordinary pubs to an ever-growing number of branded houses, including T. & J. Bernard, Barras & Co., Chef & Brewer, Old Orleans and Rat & Parrot. Within three years, Brian Stewart forecast, two-thirds of Scottish & Newcastle's pubs would be operating under a brand name. 'The quality of our pubs and restaurants is a complex amalgam of their locations, their buildings, their decor and furnishings, the food and beverages they offer, and above all the character of the staff,' Stewart explained. Branding was the best way to ensure the ever-higher standards of friendliness and efficiency that would be needed to ensure that Scottish & Newcastle obtained and maintained a leading place in the British retail sector.

The value of high-quality brands was equally obvious in the leisure division, by then led by John Dalgety, although it had to be admitted that the price of continued success was a never-ending effort to match the expectations of consumers.

And the same was true of the beer market, where Guy Dickson, the new chairman of Scottish Courage, was focusing on unremitting improvement and persistent promotion of the group's major brands.

The good news was that so far the strategy was paying off. Two hundred and fifty years after William Younger made his first tentative step into the brewing industry, Scottish & Newcastle had become the

This book comes with free EN-gage online resources so that you can study anytime, anywhere. This free online resource is not sold separately and is included in the price of the book.

How to access your online resources

You can access additional online resources associated with this CIMA Official book via the EN-gage website at: **www.EN-gage.co.uk/addabook**.

Existing users

If you are an **existing EN-gage user**, simply log-in to your account using the address above, which will enable you to use the 'add a book' menu. Enter the ISBN of this book and the unique pass key number in the scratch panel below to gain access to the extra online products.

New users

If you are a new EN-gage user then you will first need to register at: **www.EN-gage.co.uk**. Once registered, Kaplan Publishing will send you an email containing a link to activate your account - please check your junk mail if you do not receive this or contact us using the details printed on the back cover of this book. Click on the link to activate your account.

To unlock your additional resources, go to **www.EN-gage.co.uk/addabook**. You will then need to enter the ISBN of this book (found on page ii or the back cover) and the unique pass key number contained in the scratch panel below:

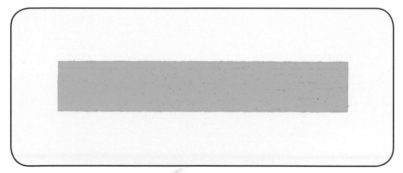

Then click 'finished' or 'add another book'.

Please allow 24 hours from the time you submit your book details for the content to appear in your account.

Your code and information

This code can only be used once for the registration of one book online. This registration will expire when this edition of the book is no longer current - please see the back cover of this book for the expiry date.

Using your online resources during your studies

All of the free online resources have been designed to support your studies. The extra online testing provides valuable question practice prior to your assessment and therefore we strongly recommend using this alongside this book.